# DISNEYLAND COOKBOOK

By Florine Sikking and Judith Zeidler

Armstrong Publishing

First Printing, April 1976

© 1976 Walt Disney Productions

Library of Congress Catalog Card Number: 76-2332
Printed in the United States of America

All rights reserved
ISBN 0-915936-02-X

Recipes created especially
for the "Disneyland Cookbook"
by: Brentwood Culinary Consultants
   HOME ECONOMISTS

Published by:
   Armstrong Publishing Company
   5514 Wilshire Boulevard
   Los Angeles, California 90036

Table of Contents

INTRODUCTION	9-10
FANTASYLAND RECIPES	11-28
MAIN STREET RECIPES	29-46
ADVENTURELAND RECIPES	47-64
TOMORROWLAND RECIPES	65-82
NEW ORLEANS SQUARE RECIPES	83-100
FRONTIERLAND RECIPES	101-118
INDEX	121-124
METRIC CONVERSION	126
TABLE OF MEASUREMENTS	127

Walt Disney's personal recipe for happiness was unique, a combination of daring creativity and inspiration—sprinkled with joy, seasoned with warmth and sweetened with unmeasured love and laughter. All of these happy ingredients blended together perfectly to become the magical delight known as DISNEYLAND.

We've faithfully followed Walt Disney's happy formula in this unique gathering of many kinds of flavors and tastes designed for universal appeal. These new and original recipes are delightfully different, entertaining to read, fun to make—something to savor and remember for days after tasting their delicious results. With DISNEYLAND as its first name, you wouldn't expect anything less in a cookbook, would you?

As in Disneyland itself, our DISNEYLAND COOK-

BOOK has a distinct flavor for each and every possible taste—Adventureland for the bold, Main Street, U.S.A. for the traditional, New Orleans Square for the gracious, Tomorrowland for the eternal optimist, Frontierland for the inquisitive and Fantasyland for the dreamer.

Regional specialties are included, because they are something special from a special place. The recipes are easy to read, simple to make, although some may seem complex or extravagant. Others are deceptively short and sweet, but the result is strikingly novel. Most are somewhere in between, but all are proven and well worth your testing—that's why they carry the Disneyland banner.

The new DISNEYLAND COOKBOOK, something special just for you.

FANTASYLAND

FANTASYLAND—where carefree dreams always do come true—is Disneyland's happiest land of all. Classic stories of childhood are brought to life as thrilling adventures for youngsters—from *Dumbo Flying Elephants* to *Peter Pan Flight* to *Alice in Wonderland*. Above all, a love for laughter is highlighted by *It's a Small World*—a musical fantasy featuring the songs and costumes of youngsters from more than 100 nations. Yes, our Fantasyland recipes are as happy and carefree as a daring ride in a *Matterhorn Bobsled*.

White Rabbit's Cabbage Soup

Hearty and robust, this Hungarian-style soup/stew is marvelous with thick slices of pumpernickel bread. An entire meal in itself.

- 5 pounds brisket of beef
- 3 pounds shin bone
- 1 bay leaf, crumbled
- 2 cloves garlic
- 1 medium onion, halved
- 5 tablespoons parsley, chopped
- 1 cabbage, coarsely shredded
- 3 onions, chopped
- 1 16-ounce can tomatoes or 6 fresh tomatoes
- 3 large beets, peeled and diced
- juice of 6 lemons
- 3 tablespoons brown sugar
- ⅛ teaspoon paprika
- ½ teaspoon basil
- ¼ teaspoon celery salt
- salt and pepper
- ½ cup sour cream

In a large pot, put meat and bones and cover with water. Add a bay leaf, garlic, onion and parsley. Bring to a boil slowly. Skim froth from the top of the mixture. Reduce heat, let simmer covered for 2 hours. Cool, then refrigerate several hours. Discard surface fat. With a slotted spoon, remove meat and bones and set aside. Strain stock and return liquid to pot and reheat gradually. Add cabbage, chopped onions, tomatoes and beets. Stir in lemon juice, sugar, paprika, basil, celery salt and salt and pepper to taste. Add meat to soup and about 2 cups of boiling water if needed. Simmer for 1 hour. Taste and add more sugar or lemon juice to taste.

Before serving, remove bones and slice brisket. Place meat in each individual soup bowl and ladle in soup. Top with a dollop of sour cream and sprinkle with paprika.

Serves 6-8

Won Ton Soup

Probably the most well-known Chinese soup, it's not difficult to do it yourself. The filled Won Ton can also be deep fried in hot oil and served as an hors d'oeuvre.

Won Ton skins

If wonton skins are unavailable, you can easily make your own.

- 1 cup all-purpose flour
- ½ teaspoon salt
- 1 egg, beaten

Combine flour and salt in a sifter and sift into a bowl. Add the egg and knead until thoroughly mixed. Turn dough out onto a floured board and knead until smooth. Cover dough with a wet towel and let stand for 20 minutes. Roll dough out paper thin and cut into 4-inch squares.

Filling:

- ½ pound ground pork, chicken or shrimp
- ½ teaspoon salt
- ½ teaspoon sugar
- 1 stalk celery, chopped fine
- 1 scallion, chopped fine
- 1 tablespoon dry sherry
- 1 tablespoon soy sauce

Combine all ingredients and mix thoroughly. To make wonton, place a half teaspoon of filling in the center of each wonton skin. Fold skin in half, pressing edges together and in half again lengthwise. Pull the two corners (edges) together to form a "nurse's hat" and seal edges with a few drops of water.

(Note: these wonton can now be frozen in a tightly sealed plastic bag.)

Yields: 16 wontons

Continued on next page

Soup:
- 3 cups chicken broth
- 2 stalks celery, sliced thin diagonally
- 1 tablespoon soy sauce
- ½ teaspoon salt
- white pepper to taste
- 1 scallion, sliced thin

Bring 3 quarts of water to a boil and drop in wontons and boil again. Wontons will float to surface when done. Add ½ cup of cold water and bring to a boil. Remove wontons with a slotted spoon and reserve. Heat chicken broth with celery, soy sauce, salt and pepper. When just to the boil, gently add wontons and scallions.
Serves 4

Mushrooms and Pears, Vinegarette

The Anjou pear, from France, combines harmoniously with fresh, sliced mushrooms. This dish can be served after the entree, to refresh the palate before dessert.

- 3 pears
- 1½ cups fresh mushrooms, sliced
- ¼ cup lemon juice
- 3 tablespoons water
- ½ cup vegetable oil
- ¼ teaspoon pepper
- ⅓ cup parsley, chopped
- 1 teaspoon onion, grated
- ¾ teaspoon salt
- 1 teaspoon sugar
- 3 sprigs watercress, stems removed

Peel, core and slice pears and combine with mushrooms. In a separate bowl, combine remaining ingredients and pour over pears and mushrooms. Cover and refrigerate 3 hours or more. Before serving, add watercress and toss gently. Serve on a bed of crisp lettuce.
Serves 4

Steamed Buns

A novel Sunday brunch dish in the United States is this version of the traditional Chinese teacake. It's also good in place of a hamburger for the children's lunch.

Buns:
- 1 package dry yeast
- water
- 4½ cups all-purpose flour
- ½ cup honey
- 1 teaspoon salt
- 1½ cups lukewarm water
- 1 tablespoon vegetable oil
- 2 cups filling

Dissolve yeast in ½ cup warm water and set aside.

In a large mixing bowl add 1 cup lukewarm water, oil and honey and mix together. Add yeast mixture. Add flour until soft dough is formed. Turn out onto a floured board and knead for about 5 minutes. Place in a greased bowl in warm place and let rise for 1½ hours until double in bulk.

Pinch off plum-size pieces of dough and flatten on a bread board. Place 1 tablespoon filling in center and pull dough up over filling and pinch edges together. Place pinched side down on a 2 x 2 inch square of wax paper on a cookie sheet. Cover and let rise in a warm place until doubled in size (about 1½ hours).

Place buns in a large pot on a rack above boiling water. Cover and steam for 15 minutes. Serve hot. Can be reheated by steaming over boiling water for about 5 minutes.

Instead of steaming, they can also be baked in a preheated 375° oven for 15 minutes.
Yields 2 dozen

Filling:
- 1 cup chicken, cooked and shredded (or cooked meat or shrimp)
- ¼ cup mushrooms, chopped
- ¼ cup bamboo shoots, chopped
- ¼ cup water chestnuts, chopped
- ¼ cup green onions, sliced
- 2 tablespoons hoisin sauce (or soy sauce)

Combine all ingredients and mix thoroughly.

Fig Loaf

Here's an outstanding Mediterranean-type recipe that answers the question of how to use fresh figs to best advantage.

- 1¼ cups all-purpose flour
- 1 cup sugar
- 1 teaspoon baking soda
- ½ teaspoon salt
- ½ cup shortening
- 1 cup walnuts, chopped
- 1 cup fresh figs, peeled & mashed**
- 2 eggs
- ¼ cup buttermilk (or regular milk)

Sift together first four ingredients in a mixing bowl. Add shortening and beat until crumbly. With a wooden spoon, mix in walnuts. Set aside.

In another bowl, combine mashed figs, eggs and buttermilk and mix with a fork or wire whisk. Add this mixture all at once to flour mixture. Mix gently until all dry particles are moistened. Do not over mix.

Spoon batter into 2 medium, greased and lightly floured loaf pans.* Sprinkle 1 tablespoon of Crumb Topping on each loaf.

Bake in a preheated 350° oven for 45 minutes or until toothpick comes out dry. Remove loaves from pans and set on wire racks to cool.

Crumb Topping:
- ½ cup brown sugar
- ¼ cup all-purpose flour
- ¼ cup butter, unsalted
- ½ teaspoon cinnamon
- ½ cup walnuts, chopped

Combine all ingredients except walnuts and blend thoroughly. Add walnuts.

**Dried figs can be substituted, cutting tough stems off and discarding. Place figs in blender and puree.

*Pan sizes: 3½x7½x2 use 2 pans
　　　　　 5x9x3 use 1 pan
　　　　　 3x5x2 use 4 pans

Spinach Canneloni

Unlike the usual canneloni pasta, the corn meal adds flavor and body to this Italian-style crepe. It's terrific to feature for a buffet dinner or large group since it can be prepared well in advance.

Crepe:
- ½ cup corn meal
- ½ cup sifted all-purpose flour
- 1½ teaspoons salt
- 3 eggs
- 1½ cups milk
- 1 tablespoon butter or margarine

Combine all ingredients and mix until smooth and thoroughly blended. Heat butter in a small skillet and rotate pan to evenly spread butter. Pour in enough batter to just coat bottom of pan, rotating pan to spread evenly. When batter begins to leave sides of pan, gently lift and turn over. Cook for 1 minute and drop crepe out on a board. Continue making crepes until all batter is used. Be sure to stir batter from bottom before pouring into pan.

Filling:
- 2 cups fresh spinach, chopped (or 3 boxes frozen spinach, chopped)
- 2 cups ricotta cheese
- 5 tablespoons butter
- 5 tablespoons Parmesan cheese
- ½ teaspoon marjoram, crushed
- 1 teaspoon thyme, crushed
- salt and pepper to taste

Combine all ingredients and mix thoroughly. Spoon 3 heaping tablespoons of spinach filling 1 inch from the edge of the crepe and roll once. Fold over edges to seal and continue rolling. Place in a glass baking dish. (Should you wish to freeze these canneloni, line a box with wax paper and place the canneloni in layers with wax paper between each layer.)

Yields 2 dozen

Continued on next page

Sauce:
- 2 tablespoons vegetable oil
- 1 medium onion, chopped
- ½ tablespoon all-purpose flour
- 3 8-ounce cans tomato sauce
- 2 cups beef or chicken stock
- ¾ cup Parmesan cheese
- 1 teaspoon sugar
- salt and pepper to taste

Heat oil in a large skillet and saute onion until soft. Add flour and blend into a paste. Slowly pour in tomato sauce, mixing constantly. Add remaining ingredients and blend thoroughly.

Spoon sauce on bottom of baking dish just to coat. Using two canneloni per person, place cahneloni in a baking dish and pour sauce over each canneloni. Bake in 350° oven for 45 minutes. Freeze unused canneloni and sauce separately.

Prince John's Yorkshire Pudding

One always associates this traditional English dish with roast beef. Not necessarily so here, as this recipe couples as well with the Veal in Foil found in this section.

- 1 cup sifted all-purpose flour
- ½ teaspoon salt
- 1 cup light cream or milk
- 2 large whole eggs
- 1 tablespoon beef suet (ground fine)

Combine sifted flour and salt, slowly stir in light cream and beef suet and mix well together. Transfer the mixture to the container of a blender or electric mixer, add eggs and blend the batter until it is creamy. Chill for at least 15 minutes. Preheat muffin pan in 450° oven for 3 minutes. Brush well with beef drippings from roast or use vegetable oil and fill muffin cups about ¾ full. Bake in a 450° oven for about 15 minutes then reduce the temperature to 350° and bake for about 15 minutes longer or until it is light, crisp and brown. (Note: Be sure it is brown all around or it will fall.)

Yields 6

Eggplant and Tomato Pie

Typical Italian ingredients are combined to create this spectacular new pie. Serve as a main dish or as a vegetable.

1 10-inch pie shell, unbaked (see Main Street's "Apple Pie")

Filling:
- 1½ pounds eggplant
- salt
- ⅔ cup vegetable oil
- black pepper
- ¼ pound mushrooms, fresh or canned, drained
- 3 eggs
- 1½ cups tomato puree (see recipe following)
- 2 tablespoons fresh basil, chopped (or 1 teaspoon dried)
- 2 tablespoons fresh parsley, chopped (or 1 teaspoon dried)
- 3 tablespoons Parmesan cheese, grated
- 4 tablespoons French-style mustard

Peel the eggplant and cut in ½-inch pieces. Spread out on paper towels and sprinkle with salt. Let stand for 15 minutes; turn and salt and let stand for an additional 15 minutes. Rinse in strainer or colander and spread out on paper towels and pat dry. Heat oil in frying pan and saute eggplant over medium heat until soft and lightly browned. Chop mushrooms fine and add to eggplant. Season with salt and pepper and set aside. Beat eggs in a large mixing bowl. Add the tomato puree, chopped herbs, salt and pepper and mix thoroughly. Fold in the eggplant. (Mixture can be refrigerated until ready for baking.)

Fill unbaked pie shell with wax paper and rice to weigh it down. Bake pie shell for 5 to 10 minutes in 350° oven. Remove from oven and cool. Brush bottom of pastry shell with mustard; return to oven for 10 more minutes. Remove from oven and cool. Fill with eggplant and tomato mixture. Sprinkle with Parmesan cheese. Bake in 375° oven for 30 minutes or until top is set. Serve immediately.

Serves 6-8

Tomato Puree:
- 5 pounds tomatoes (or 3 large cans whole tomatoes)
- 4 tablespoons vegetable oil
- 2 onions, minced
- 4 garlic cloves, chopped
- bouquet garni: 1 teaspoon each thyme, basil, oregano
- salt and pepper
- 2 tablespoons sugar

Continued on next page

Peel and cut tomatoes. In a large skillet, heat 2 tablespoons oil. Add tomatoes and cook until tender, stirring occasionally. Put through a blender and set aside.

In the same skillet, heat additional 2 tablespoons oil and add onions. Cook until tender. Add pureed tomatoes, garlic and bouquet garni (thyme, basil and oregano tied together in cheesecloth) and bring to a simmer. Simmer for 15 minutes.

Remove the bouquet garni and puree mixture again. Strain into skillet, add salt, pepper and sugar to taste and simmer 10-15 minutes, stirring occasionally. At this point, if the sauce is too liquid, simmer a little longer until of desired consistency.

Refrigerate or freeze unused puree in one-cup portions. Enhances spaghetti sauce, stews and any recipe using a tomato puree.

Yields: 3 cups

Veal In Foil

Similar to a Swiss dish, veal prepared like this can be found in the countryside. Sharpen your carving knife as this meat is delectable when sliced thin.

- 6 pound veal shoulder
- 1 onion, sliced
- 1 pound carrots, halved
- 10 small onions
- 12 small mushrooms
- salt and pepper
- 1 teaspoon rosemary
- 1 teaspoon thyme
- 1 cup chicken stock

In a shallow pan, place a large sheet of heavy-duty foil long enough to cover veal and vegetables. Place veal in center of foil over sliced onion, fat side up. Brown meat under broiler for 3 to 5 minutes. Remove from oven and surround meat with carrots, small onions and mushrooms. Sprinkle with salt and pepper, rosemary and thyme. Spoon chicken stock over meat. Seal foil securely so no air escapes. Place in a preheated 350° oven for 2 hours. Uncover or open foil and fold back and continue baking until tender. Slice thin and serve hot surrounded by vegetables.

Serves 8-10

Gravlax with Dill Sauce
(Salmon Marinated in Dill)

Cured the way the Scandinavians do it, this salmon is easily made to serve as your first course. This great dill sauce refrigerates well and improves any fish dish.

- 4 pounds fresh salmon
- ¼ cup coarse salt (kosher)
- ¼ cup sugar
- 2 tablespoons peppercorns, crushed
- 1 large bunch dill, fresh

Cut salmon in half, lengthwise, and remove the backbone and small bones. In a bowl combine the salt, sugar and crushed peppercorns. Set aside. Wash and shake dry the bunch of dill and set aside.

In a long glass baking dish, place half of the fish skin side down. Sprinkle salt mixture over fish. Place dill on top. Place other half of fish, cut side down, over dill. Cover with plastic wrap and foil. Pile 3 or 4 heavy cans of food on foil to weight the fish down. Refrigerate.

Every 12 hours, remove from refrigerator. Uncover and baste with liquid that has accumulated, inside and out. Turn the fish over so the bottom is now on top and the top is on the bottom. Cover again and refrigerate. Repeat this for 3 or 4 days.

When ready to serve, remove the fish from the glass dish. Remove the dill and scrape away the seasonings. Place the separate halves, skin side down, on a wooden board and slice as thin as possible on the diagonal, but not cutting through to the skin. Serve several slices on each plate with a dollop of dill sauce, garnish with sprig of fresh dill.

This can be refrigerated for several days or frozen and defrosted several hours before using.

Serves 16

Dill Sauce:
- 2 tablespoons sugar
- 1 tablespoon white vinegar
- 3 tablespoons dark mustard
- 1 teaspoon dry mustard
- ⅓ cup vegetable oil
- 3 tablespoons fresh chopped dill

In a small, deep bowl, mix the sugar, vinegar and two mustards into a paste. With a wire whisk, slowly beat in the oil until it forms a thick mayonnaise. Stir in the chopped dill. This can be refrigerated for several days, covered with plastic wrap.

Yields: ½ cup

Chicken Turnovers

Have you ever had chicken with powdered sugar and cinnamon the Moroccan way? If not, try this out-of-the-ordinary recipe and taste what you've been missing.

- 1½ cups almonds, chopped
- 3 tablespoons butter, unsalted
- ⅓ cup onion, minced
- 3 garlic cloves, crushed
- 3 tablespoons butter, unsalted
- 9 eggs
- 3 tablespoons parsley, chopped
- 1½ teaspoons salt
- 1 teaspoon pepper
- 6 tablespoons sugar
- 2 teaspoons cinnamon
- ½ teaspoon ground ginger
- ¼ teaspoon nutmeg
- Mock Puff Pastry (see Main Street's Rutabaga and Carrot Puffs)
- 3 cups chicken, cooked and shredded

In a skillet, saute almonds in 3 tablespoons butter until golden brown and set aside in a small bowl. In same skillet, saute onions and garlic in 3 tablespoons butter until tender. Beat eggs, add parsley, salt and pepper and add to skillet. Cook over low heat, stirring until eggs are set. Set aside. Combine sugar, cinnamon, ginger and nutmeg in a small bowl and set aside.

Roll out "Mock Puff Pastry" on floured wax paper and cut six 8-inch rounds. Spoon shredded chicken on half of pastry and top with egg mixture, spreading evenly. Sprinkle sauteed almonds over eggs and add sugar mixture over almonds. Fold unfilled side of pastry over chicken mixture and seal edges. Place on buttered cookie sheet. Bake in preheated 350° oven for 25 to 30 minutes or until golden brown. Sprinkle with powdered sugar and cinnamon.

Serves 6

Goofy's Fish Mousse with Green Mayonnaise Sauce

As an elegant first course, instead of soup or salad, fish courses like this add interest to your dining. Don't be put off by the length of this recipe, do like the Dutch do and prepare it in advance.

- 1½ pounds halibut* fillet
- ½ pound butterfish* fillet
- 1 tablespoon butter, unsalted
- salt & pepper
- ½ cup fresh spinach, cooked
- 2 tablespoons butter, unsalted
- ¼ teaspoon salt
- dash pepper

- ⅓ cup mushrooms, minced (fresh or canned)
- 1 tablespoon butter
- 3 anchovy fillets
- 3 teaspoons lemon juice
- ½ cup butter, unsalted
- salt & pepper to taste
- additional anchovies for garnish

Place fish in buttered oven-proof dish, just large enough to hold fish. Spread butter on top of fish and sprinkle with salt and pepper. Cover with buttered sheet of wax paper and bake in a preheated oven 350° for 15 minutes or until flaky. Set aside.

Drain and chop the spinach and mash in the butter thoroughly then add salt and pepper. (Can substitute frozen spinach using ½ box defrosted and drained thoroughly.) Set aside.

In a skillet, saute mushrooms in 1 tablespoon butter until they are golden. Mash the anchovies in a bowl and add the mushrooms. Set aside. In a large, shallow bowl, mash the cooked fish with the pan juices. Add the mushroom mixture and lemon juice. Add the remaining butter and continue mixing until smooth. Add salt and pepper to taste. Line a 3 cup mold with plastic wrap, leaving 2 inches extra around the mold. Arrange strips of additional anchovies in an attractive design to match the design of the mold. Spoon half of the fish mousse carefully over anchovies. Spread spinach mixture over mousse and then spoon in the remaining fish mousse mixture. Cover with plastic wrap and seal with foil. Refrigerate.

To serve: Remove foil and overlapping plastic wrap and turn out onto a platter and gently remove plastic wrap. Garnish platter with parsley and slices of lemon (sprinkle lemon slices with paprika). Slice 1-inch servings and serve with green mayonnaise sauce.

*Any soft-meat fish can be used, such as trout or turbot.

Serves 6-8

Green Mayonnaise Sauce:
- 1 egg
- 5 teaspoons lemon juice
- 1 teaspoon dry mustard
- ½ teaspoon salt
- ⅛ teaspoon white pepper
- 1 cup vegetable oil
- 1 tablespoon fresh parsley, minced
- 1½ teaspoons fresh chives, minced
- 1½ teaspoons tarragon, crushed
- ½ teaspoon dill, minced
- ½ teaspoon chervil, crushed

Using a blender, electric mixer or wire whisk, mix together the egg, lemon juice, mustard, salt and white pepper. Blend in the oil, pouring it in a thick steady stream, until the whole cup is added. This is now mayonnaise.

Pour mayonnaise into a small bowl and with a wooden spoon, mix in the remaining ingredients. Cover with plastic wrap and refrigerate. Yields 1½ cups

Fantasyland Zabaglione

Whip this Franco-Italian specialty up fast when dessert is needed for unexpected company. The constant beating with a wire whisk keeps it light and frothy. Practice *does* make perfect with this seemingly simple recipe.

- 6 egg yolks
- ½ cup sugar
- ⅔ cup dry Marsala wine

Remove top from double boiler and place in it egg yolks and sugar and beat until thick and pale yellow. Gradually add Marsala wine, beating constantly.

Replace top of boiler over simmering water and continue to beat vigorously until mixture foams and begins to thicken, being careful not to overcook. (Consistency should be similar to beaten egg whites or a meringue.)

When serving hot, pour into Lacy Almond Cups (recipe in this section) and serve immediately. When serving Frozen Zabaglione, pour into a bowl and freeze. Remove from freezer and spoon into Lacy Almond Cups. Serves 6

Pear Tart with Dessert Pastry

Ordinary pears are cleverly converted into a beautiful dessert in this recipe. Any inexpensive champagne is suitable in which to poach pears in this Gallic recipe.

- 2 cups champagne
- 1¼ cups sugar
- 12 pears, peeled, cored and halved
- 1 baked "Dessert Pastry Crust"
- ½ cup crushed vanilla wafers
- 2 tablespoons kirsch or sherry
- ¼ cup grated almonds

In a 6-quart saucepan, bring champagne and 1 cup sugar to a simmer. Drop in pears and poach for 10-15 minutes or until tender but still firm. Remove pears with care and place in a large shallow baking dish and set aside. Continue simmering sauce until reduced in half and set aside.

When ready to serve, arrange pear halves, cut-side down, on baked Dessert Pastry Crust. Cover with crushed wafers. Sprinkle with kirsch or sherry and top with remaining ¼ cup sugar and grated almonds mixed together. Place in 375° oven for 5 minutes. Remove and serve with champagne sauce.

Serves 6-8

Dessert Pastry Crust:
- 1½ cups all-purpose flour
- ⅓ cup confectioners sugar
- ¼ teaspoon salt
- ½ cup butter or margarine, unsalted
- 3 tablespoons milk

In a large mixing bowl, sift together flour, sugar and salt. Add butter and with a pastry blender or electric mixer blend until coarse meal. Add milk all at once and mix until dough comes away from sides of bowl. Work with hands into a soft ball. Roll out on floured wax paper, for easier handling, about ⅛ inch thick. Gently pick up one side of wax paper and fold half of pastry over the other half. Then gently pick up folded end of dough and ease it into a 10-inch tart pan and unfold, loosely draping dough inside of tart shell. Trim dough leaving one inch to turn under for a thicker edge.

Tart can be covered with plastic wrap at this point and refrigerated or can be covered with wax paper and rice* and baked in a preheated 375° oven for 10 or 15 minutes then gently remove wax paper with rice and continue baking until bottom of pastry starts to brown lightly, or approximately 5 minutes.

Cool and fill with fruit.

Yield: 1 10-inch pie crust

*Prevents pie crust from bubbling.

Lacy Almond Cups

You're aiming for visual effect here so be careful and quick with the molding or you'll end up with almond brittle. Fill these Danish almond cups with Zabaglione, found elsewhere in this section.

- ⅔ cup almonds, ground
- ½ cup sugar
- 1 tablespoon all-purpose flour
- ½ cup butter, unsalted
- 2 tablespoons milk

In a large skillet mix together almonds, sugar and flour. Add butter and milk and cook over medium heat, stirring until butter is melted and all ingredients are combined thoroughly.

Making only 2 almond cups at a time, drop 1 teaspoon of batter onto a greased and floured cookie sheet 4 inches apart. Bake in a preheated 350° oven approximately 8 to 10 minutes until golden brown.

Allow a few seconds to set, then remove flat almond round with a metal pancake turner and carefully place it over the bottom of an upside down glass. Mold into a cup shape with fingers. Remove from glass bottom and turn almond cup right-side up on a large tray until ready to fill.

(Note: Almond rounds harden quickly after baking, so only make 2 at a time as instructed. Should they harden too quickly, return to oven for 1 minute.)

Fantasia Cheesecake

You have the option here on the final texture of this cheesecake. For a more cake-like texture bake about 10 minutes longer than called for in this recipe. And for a creamier cake, remove 5 minutes sooner.

- 4 cups (32 ounces) cream cheese
- 2 cups sugar
- ¼ teaspoon salt
- ½ teaspoon lemon flavoring
- 4 whole eggs

With an electric mixer, beat cream cheese until smooth. Gradually add sugar, blending thoroughly. Add salt and lemon flavoring and mix well. Add one egg at a time, blending thoroughly after each addition. Set aside.

Graham Cracker Crust:
- 1 cup graham cracker meal
- 1 tablespoon granulated sugar
- ¼ cup butter or margarine, softened
- 1 cup sour cream
- 2 tablespoons sugar

Combine first three ingredients and blend thoroughly. Press into a greased 9-inch spring form or cake pan. Pour in cheese mixture and bake in preheated 350° oven for 1 hour and 10 minutes, or until golden on top. Cool thoroughly. If you have used a cake pan, place a board the same size as cake on top, then tip slightly until loose and turn over on a dish.

Combine sour cream and sugar and spread evenly on top of cheesecake. For variety, top the cake with fresh strawberries or any other pie fruit filling. Make a border of whipping cream.

MAIN STREET, USA

MAIN STREET, U.S.A. — where a Turn-of-the-Century American home town is authentically recreated — is the stepping off point for a magical journey into the many worlds of Disneyland. This introductory atmosphere transports you back to the slower-paced era of 1900. Here you recapture the nostalgia of by-gone years with a real horseless carriage, gas lamps, silent movies, a penny arcade, a band concert in Town Square — all rekindling fond memories of a more friendly way of life. This tradition and heritage are featured in our recipes of yesterday — remodeled for today.

1900's Tomato Cream Soup

Nobody makes home-made tomato soup anymore — and that's a shame. Because it's really better, and even better for you, than anything out of a can.

- 8 ripe tomatoes or 2 1-pound 12-ounce cans tomatoes, well drained
- 2 tablespoons onion, chopped
- 2 tablespoons celery, chopped
- 1 bay leaf, crushed
- 3 whole cloves
- 1 sprig parsley
- 2 cups half-and-half
- 1 cup milk
- ¼ cup butter, unsalted
- ¼ cup all-purpose flour
- 1½ teaspoons salt
- ¼ teaspoon pepper
- Garnish: 2 tablespoons chopped tomato and 2 tablespoons parsley

Peel, puree and strain fresh tomatoes. Place tomato puree in a saucepan with onions and celery. Fill a 4-inch square piece of cheesecloth with bay leaf, cloves and parsley and tie with a string, making a sack. Bring to a boil and simmer for 10 to 15 minutes. Remove sack of herbs and puree tomato mixture in a blender, then set aside. In the same saucepan bring half-and-half and milk to a simmer and set aside. In another saucepan melt butter, add flour and blend with a wire whisk. Add the milk mixture and continue stirring with wire whisk until thick. Add salt and pepper. Pour a little of the milk mixture into the tomato puree, blending with wire whisk to keep from curdling. Then pour the entire tomato puree mixture into the milk mixture, stirring constantly. Serve hot, garnish with tomatoes and parsley.

(When reheating, bring to a simmer, stirring constantly with a wire whisk.)
Serves 6

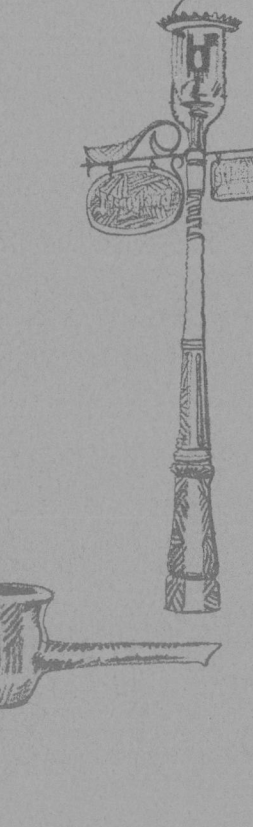

Old-Fashioned Corn Soup

Melted cheese and popcorn! If this doesn't make your children sit up and ask for more, nothing (except dessert) will.

- 2 tablespoons chopped onion
- 3 tablespoons butter
- 3 tablespoons all-purpose flour
- 2½ cups corn (cream style)
- 1½ cups chicken stock
- 1½ cups milk
- salt and pepper to taste
- ½ cup heavy cream
- 1 cup Monterey jack cheese, cut in ½-inch cubes
- ½ cup popcorn, popped
- chopped chives

In a saucepan, saute onion in butter until soft. Add flour and cook for 2 minutes. Add corn, stock and milk and bring to a simmer. Cook 5 minutes, stirring occasionally. Add salt and pepper and cream. Heat. When ready to serve, add cheese cubes. Ladle into cups and garnish with popcorn and chives.

Serves 6

Tuna Salad with Curry and Almonds

It's the pinch of curry that does it. The pimientos add color and the almonds add the crunch.

- 1 7-ounce can tuna, well drained
- 2 eggs, hard cooked and chopped
- 2 stalks celery, chopped
- 1 2-ounce jar pimientos, drained and sliced
- ½ cup almonds, blanched and sliced
- ¼ cup mayonnaise
- ⅛ teaspoon curry
- ½ teaspoon capers

Flake tuna in a mixing bowl and add eggs, celery, pimientos and almonds. In a small bowl, combine remaining ingredients and blend well. Pour mayonnaise mixture over tuna mixture and toss gently until thoroughly blended. Chill several hours. Serve on lettuce garnished with pimientos and watercress.

Serves 4-6

Wooden Barrel Dill Pickles

Dill pickles don't grow on bushes, so here's a fool-proof way to make your own. Sliced thin, they're great as a garnish.

- 1 gallon jar
- 3 tablespoons pickle spices
- 3 cloves garlic
- enough cucumbers to fill jar (approximately 10 to 12)
- 4 heaping tablespoons kosher (coarse) salt
- 3 cloves garlic
- 1 package fresh dill
- **water to cover**

Pour boiling water in jar to clean. Pour out. Drop pickle spices and garlic in bottom of jar. Place cucumbers in jar just to neck. Top with salt, garlic and dill. Add water and cover securely. Shake up and down and let stand for 3 to 4 days before serving.

Yields approximately: 10 to 12 pickles depending on size

Green tomatoes can be substituted for pickles

Pop-Up Bread

There's no "knead" to be afraid of baking this bread. It takes only two steps, then pop it out of the oven and serve hot. Goes nicely with the 1900's Tomato Cream Soup in this section.

- 3½ cups all-purpose flour
- 1 package dry yeast
- ½ cup milk
- ½ cup water
- ½ cup oil
- ¼ cup sugar
- 1 teaspoon salt
- 2 eggs

In a large mixing bowl place 1½ cups of flour and the yeast and mix together. In a saucepan, heat milk, water, oil, sugar and salt over low heat until warm, and stir to blend. Add to flour mixture and beat until smooth. Add eggs one at a time. Stir in remaining flour until dough is smooth and elastic. Spoon into 2 well-greased 1-pound coffee cans or 2 7½" x 3½" loaf pans. Cover with towel and let rise in warm place for 1 hour or until dough is ½-inch from top of coffee can. Bake in preheated 375° oven for 30 to 40 minutes. Cool in can for 10 minutes. (If bread is difficult to remove from can, take off bottom lid with a can opener and gently push bread out.)

Yields 2 loaves

Yankee Pot Roast

This main course for every Main Street all across the country is everybody's good old standby. Try this version with the Natural Health Food Salad in the Tomorrowland section or the Zucchini Salad in the Adventureland section. And end it all with our Apple Pie here in Main Street.

- 2 onions, sliced
- ½ green pepper
- 2 stalks celery
- parsley
- 8 carrots, cut in large chunks
- 2 cloves garlic, chopped
- 6 pounds boneless roast (rump or shoulder)
- herbs - 1 bay leaf, ¼ teaspoon each oregano, basil, thyme
- salt to taste
- 8 peppercorns
- 1 8-ounce can tomato sauce
- 1 cup dry red wine
- 3 medium potatoes, peeled and cut in large chunks

In a large roaster layer 1 onion, green pepper, celery, parsley, carrots and garlic. Place roast on top; sprinkle with remaining onions and herbs, salt, peppercorns, tomato sauce and wine. Cover and roast in preheated 350° oven for 2 hours until tender. Baste every 20 minutes. Add potatoes and cook an additional hour.

Serves 10-12

Rutabaga and Carrot Puffs

It's best as a vegetable/starch, but also appropriate as an hors d'oeuvre. Totally unique, it's fun to make, serve, and talk about. Can be frozen before baking and popped into the oven whenever needed for unexpected company.

- 3 cups all-purpose flour
- 1 teaspoon baking powder
- 1 teaspoon sugar
- 1 teaspoon salt
- ½ cup butter, unsalted
- 1 egg
- 1 cup sour cream

- 2 large rutabagas, sliced
- 12 carrots, sliced
- 2 tablespoons sugar
- 1 teaspoon salt
- 2 tablespoons butter

Place flour, baking powder, sugar, salt and butter in a large mixing bowl. Blend until crumbly. Add egg and sour cream and beat until thoroughly blended. Wrap with wax paper and refrigerate, or freeze until ready to use.

Put rutabaga, carrots, sugar and salt in a saucepan, cover with water, bring to a boil and simmer until soft—about 15 minutes. Drain and puree in blender. Add 1 tablespoon butter and mix well. Cool. Roll out pastry on a floured board and cut in 3-inch circles. Place one teaspoon of puree on each circle and seal closed with floured fingertips. Press sealed edge with fork and place on greased cookie sheet. Bake in preheated 375° oven for 15 minutes or until golden brown. Serve at once.

Yields 24

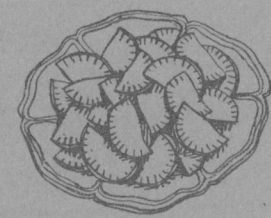

Macaroni and Cheese Souffle

Delight your children with this variation of an old favorite. Macaroni and cheese never had it so good!

- 1 8-ounce package elbow macaroni
- ½ cup butter, unsalted
- 3 tablespoons all-purpose flour
- 1½ teaspoons salt
- ¼ teaspoon white pepper
- 2 cups milk
- ½ cup cream
- ⅔ cup grated Parmesan cheese (or cheddar cheese)
- 3 egg yolks
- 5 egg whites, stiffly beaten

Drop macaroni in boiling water and cook until tender. Drain and set aside.

In a heavy saucepan, melt ¼ cup butter and blend in flour, salt and pepper. Combine milk and cream and stir until the mixture comes to a boil. Simmer for 5 minutes longer. Add remaining ¼ cup butter and cheese and stir until melted. Remove from heat and set aside.

In a large bowl beat the egg yolks until light. Add the cheese mixture in a thin stream to the yolk mixture, stirring constantly with a wire whisk to prevent curdling. Add the cooked elbow macaroni, mixing thoroughly. Cool.

Beat egg whites until stiff and fold into the macaroni mixture, very gently but thoroughly. Pour into a buttered 2-quart souffle dish and bake in a preheated 375° oven for 25 to 30 minutes or until brown and set.

Serves 6-8

Potato and Mushroom Casserole

Here's a super, original recipe that really goes great with plain old hamburger. And believe it or not, it's just as tasty and moist when reheated the next day.

- 5 medium potatoes, sliced thin
- ¼ teaspoon salt
- ¼ teaspoon pepper
- 4 tablespoons butter
- ¼ teaspoon garlic salt
- 1½ pounds mushrooms, sliced (fresh or canned)
- 1 cup grated Swiss cheese
- ½ cup minced parsley
- 3 green onions, minced
- 1 pint heavy cream

Mix potatoes, salt and pepper. Blend butter and garlic salt, and butter a 3-quart casserole generously. Put in one layer of potatoes and one layer of mushrooms. Sprinkle with cheese, parsley and onions. Continue repeating layers until all ingredients are used. Finish with a layer of potatoes. Pour cream over all, sprinkle with cheese and bits of butter. Bake in a moderate oven, 375° for 1 hour, or until potatoes are done.

Serves 8

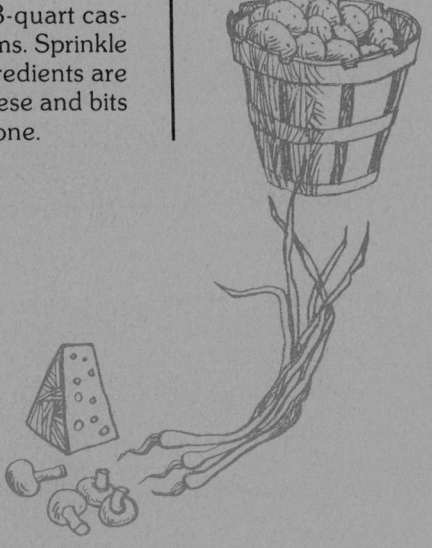

Pizza

For family fun, make this novel top-it-yourself pizza. Put out bowls of topping ingredients — pepperoni, mushrooms, anchovies and your own favorites — and let everyone go to it.

- 2 packages dry yeast
- 1¼ cups lukewarm water
- ⅛ teaspoon sugar
- ¾ cup olive oil
- 3½ cups all-purpose flour
- 1 teaspoon salt
- corn meal

Sprinkle yeast in ¼ cup lukewarm water. Add sugar and set aside.

In a large mixing bowl add 1 cup lukewarm water, yeast mixture and oil. Add flour with salt, 1 cup at a time, until thoroughly blended. Place dough on a floured board and knead about 10 to 15 minutes until smooth, shiny and elastic. Place in a large greased bowl, grease top, cover with a towel, and keep in a warm place for 1½ hours or until double in bulk.

Punch dough down, divide in fourths. Roll out on a floured board to a 10-inch round, place on pizza pan or cookie sheet that has been sprinkled with corn meal and flute edge, to prevent sauce from running out.

Spoon on sauce, sprinkle with ½ cup grated mozzarella and 3 tablespoons grated Parmesan cheese.

Bake in a preheated 500° oven for 15 minutes or until cheese has melted and crust is brown.

Makes 4 10-inch pizzas

Pizza Sauce:
- 3 tablespoons olive oil
- 1 cup onions, chopped
- 1 tablespoon garlic, chopped
- 4 cups tomatoes, chopped not drained
- 1 6-ounce can tomato paste
- 1 tablespoon oregano, crumbled
- 1 teaspoon basil
- 1 bay leaf
- 2 teaspoons sugar
- 1 tablespoon salt
- dash of pepper

Heat oil in a large saucepan, add onions and garlic, and cook until soft. Add remaining ingredients and simmer 10 minutes.

Continued on next page

Fried Fish Fritters

Here's a nifty way to use up that leftover fish that you never know what to do with. Like the fish in English "fish and chips" eat these fritters with your fingers as a main course. Try it teamed up with the Potato and Mushroom Casserole in this section.

- 3 eggs, separated
- 3 tablespoons all-purpose flour
- ½ teaspoon salt
- ⅛ teaspoon pepper
- ⅛ teaspoon garlic powder
- ½ teaspoon onion powder
- 2 cups fish, boned, cooked, flaked
- 2 cups vegetable oil

Beat egg yolks until light, add flour and seasonings, then add fish. Beat egg whites until stiff and fold into fish mixture. Drop by teaspoon into hot oil (360°) and fry until golden on all sides. Don't crowd in pot. Remove with a slotted spoon and drain on paper towels. Serve with cocktail sauce.

Yields 24

Turkey with Apple and Raisin Stuffing

For a truly juicy turkey, place it in a supermarket brown paper bag, put it in the oven, and forget about it. For variations in stuffing turkey cooked this way, try any of our other dressings.

Preparing turkey:
- 1 turkey (10 to 20 pounds)
- vegetable oil, salt, pepper, garlic, paprika
- 1 large brown paper bag

Clean turkey, pat dry with paper towels. Rub outside with oil, salt, pepper, garlic and paprika. Set aside.

Stuffing:
- ½ cup butter
- 2 cups onions, chopped
- 6 slices white bread, cubed
- 8 slices pumpernickel, cubed
- 4 apples or pears
- 1 cup raisins (plumped in wine or apple juice)
- 1 teaspoon salt
- ¼ teaspoon pepper

Melt 4 tablespoons of butter in skillet, add onions and cook until soft. Add bread and additional butter. Cook until brown, stirring with a wooden spoon. Add apples, raisins, salt and pepper and toss. Continue cooking for 5 or 10 minutes.

Fill turkey cavity with stuffing and close with needle and thread or skewers. Grease seamless section of paper bag inside and place turkey, neck first, breast side down on greased section. Fold open end of bag and seal with paper clips or staples. Place on a rack over foil-lined pan and bake in preheated 325° oven for 3 hours or more depending on size of bird. (25 minutes to the pound.)

One half hour before turkey is done, make a slit in the bag under the turkey to catch the juices in the pan and remove paper bag. Pour collected juices into a saucepan and set aside. When cool remove fat. Return turkey to oven to brown for remaining cooking time.

Continued on next page

Giblet Sauce for Gravy:
- giblets and neck
- 1 onion, sliced
- 3 carrots, chunked
- 1 parsnip (optional), chunked
- 2 celery stalks, chunked
- 3 sprigs parsley, chopped
- 1 cup white wine (dry)
- ½ teaspoon salt
- ¼ teaspoon pepper

In a heavy saucepan, place giblets, neck and vegetables with enough water and 1 cup wine to cover, salt and pepper, and simmer for 1 hour. Uncover and reduce to 1 cup. Add to pan juices in saucepan and serve in gravy bowl with turkey.

Suggested cooking time: 10-12 pounds (stuffed) - 3½ to 4½ hours
         14-16 pounds (stuffed) - 5 to 6 hours
         18-20 pounds (stuffed) - 6 to 7½ hours

Main Street Popovers

Every recipe we've ever seen tells you to bake popovers in a preheated oven. Not so here! Follow these easy directions and you'll end up with a perfect puffy popover.

- 2 eggs, beaten
- 1 cup all-purpose flour
- ½ teaspoon salt
- 1 cup milk

In a mixing bowl, combine all ingredients and mix thoroughly. Pour batter into 8 well-oiled muffin tins. Place in a cold oven and set heat at 450°. Bake for 30 minutes. Do not open oven door until end of baking time.

Yields 8

Spaghetti Meat Sauce

If you had this at Disneyland, here's how to make it at home. Delicious on any shape pasta or noodle. Be sure to sprinkle with Parmesan cheese. Pair this spaghetti dish with our Pickled Beet Salad from the Frontierland section.

- 2 tablespoons olive oil
- 1 pound ground beef
- ¾ cup onions, chopped
- 1 clove garlic, minced
- 1 29-ounce can whole tomatoes
- 1 6-ounce can tomato paste
- 2 bay leaves
- 1 teaspoon basil
- ½ teaspoon salt
- ¼ teaspoon dry ground chili pepper
- 2 tablespoons parsley, chopped
- 2 tablespoons butter, melted
- 1 pound spaghetti pasta

Heat olive oil in a 6-quart saucepan, mix in beef, onion and garlic. Cook over high heat, stirring constantly until meat browns. Add tomatoes, tomato paste, bay leaves, basil, salt and chili pepper. Cover and cook over low heat for one-half hour, adding water if the sauce becomes too thick. Taste for seasoning. Stir in parsley and melted butter. Prepare pasta according to directions on package. Pour sauce over and serve immediately.

Yields 4 cups

Apple Pie

This is the perfect apple pie to end any meal perfectly. The bottom crust stays crisp and flaky, and the apples firm and juicy.

- 3 pounds pippin apples
- juice of 1 medium lemon
- ¾ cup sugar
- 1 teaspoon cinnamon
- pinch salt
- 4 tablespoons butter

Peel and core apples. In a large bowl, slice apples into ½-inch slices and pour in lemon juice. Line a 9-inch pie plate with half of the unbaked crust (do not prick). Combine sugar, cinnamon and salt. Layer apples, the sugar mixture and dot with butter. Continue layering until all ingredients have been used. Cover pie with remaining crust dough, sealing edges carefully. Prick top of crust and bake in a preheated 425° oven for 30 minutes. Reduce heat to 350° and continue baking for an additional 30 minutes. Remove from oven and place on a rack to cool. Can be served within 30 minutes.
Serves 8

Pie Crust (double recipe for this Apple Pie or any two-crust pie):
- 1 cup all-purpose flour
- ½ teaspoon salt
- 3 tablespoons solid vegetable shortening
- 2 tablespoons butter
- ¼ cup orange juice, chilled

Combine flour and salt and cut shortening and butter into flour with pastry blender or fork until crumbly. Add chilled juice and continue cutting until dough begins to hold together. Form dough into a ball and roll out on a well-floured board. (For a two-crust pie form 2 balls and roll each ball separately.) Dough should be no more than ¼ inch thick. Run spatula under dough and gently place in a 9-inch or 10-inch pie plate.

(For recipes that call for a baked pie crust, prick dough with fork and bake in a 375° oven for 10-12 minutes or until golden brown. Remove from oven and cool on a rack.)

Spicy Chocolate Brownies

Cinnamon and cloves spice up these brownies. For a change, top with whipped cream flavored with a dash of cinnamon, sugar and pumpkin pie spice.

- 3 squares unsweetened chocolate
- ½ cup butter
- 1 cup sugar
- 2 eggs
- 1 teaspoon vanilla
- ½ cup all-purpose flour
- ½ teaspoon baking powder
- ¼ teaspoon cinnamon
- ¼ teaspoon cloves
- ½ teaspoon salt
- 1 cup walnuts, chopped coarsely

In top of double boiler, melt chocolate. Set aside to cool but not harden.

Cream butter in a large mixing bowl, add sugar and mix until fluffy. Beat in eggs and vanilla and then add cooled chocolate. Add flour, baking powder, spices and salt and mix until well blended and creamy. Stir in walnuts and pour into a greased and floured 8-inch square baking pan. Bake in a preheated 350° oven for 30 to 35 minutes. Cool on wire rack and cut in squares.

Yields 25 squares

ADVENTURELAND

ADVENTURELAND—for us stay-at-home dreamers—is that exotic far-away place in a tropical setting where mysterious things happen and danger lurks around every bend of the river. The *Jungle Cruise* is a wonderland of nature's own design, far from civilization in remote areas of Asia and Africa. And our Adventureland recipes are especially designed to let the spirit of adventure get the best of you. Dare to be different—because our recipes do!

Jungle Mushroom Soup

Fresh mushrooms make all the difference in this mushroom soup. And when you want to make eight people happy instead of the four served by this recipe, simply double the ingredients.

- 2 tablespoons butter
- 2 tablespoons onions, chopped
- 2 tablespoons all-purpose flour
- 2 cups chicken stock
- ¾ pound mushrooms (16 mushrooms —separate stems and caps)
- 1 sprig parsley
- ½ bay leaf
- ¼ teaspoon thyme
- ½ teaspoon salt
- ¼ teaspoon pepper
- ½ cup light cream

In a saucepan heat butter, add onions and simmer on low heat until tender. Add flour and stir with wooden spoon to blend for 2 or 3 minutes—do not brown. Add chicken stock and blend thoroughly. Add sliced mushroom stems, and the parsley, bay leaf and thyme which have been tied in a cheesecloth bag. Add salt and pepper and simmer covered for 15 minutes. Remove cheesecloth bag and add sliced mushroom caps, cover and continue cooking an additional 15 minutes. The soup can be held at this point until ready to serve. Add cream to warm soup and simmer on low. Serve hot, garnished with a dollop of sour cream and sprinkled with chopped parsley.

Serves 4

Disney's Clam Chowder

This creamy white chowder, a long-time Disneyland favorite, will be yours too when you discover how easy it is to make. Filled with flavor.

- 2 slices salt pork, chopped
- 3 cups water
- 1 quart clams, drained with liquor reserved
- 3 medium potatoes, cubed
- 1 medium onion, chopped
- 1 teaspoon thyme
- 3 tablespoons butter
- 1¾ cups milk
- 1 teaspoon salt
- dash of pepper
- 6 tablespoons all-purpose flour
- ¼ cup cold water

Brown salt pork in a large saucepan. Add water, clam liquor, potatoes, onion and thyme. Cook until potatoes are almost done, about 20 minutes. Then stir in butter, milk, salt, pepper and clams. Heat but do not boil. Blend 6 tablespoons flour with ¼ cup cold water to make a smooth paste. Stir into chowder and heat, but do not boil and cook an additional 15 minutes until thick.

Yields 6-8 cups

Adventureland Marinated Eggplant

Eggplant is one of those "unloved vegetables" that most people avoid. After trying it this tasty way, you'll learn to love it and serve it often.

- ¼ cup wine vinegar
- ½ teaspoon garlic, chopped fine
- ½ teaspoon dried basil, crumbled
- ½ teaspoon dried oregano, crumbled
- ½ teaspoon salt
- ⅛ teaspoon coarsely ground pepper
- 3 quarts water
- 1 1½-pound eggplant
- ¼ cup olive oil
- 1 tablespoon capers, drained and rinsed

In a large mixing bowl, place the vinegar, garlic, basil, oregano, salt, pepper and mix thoroughly. Set aside.

In a large (5-quart) saucepan, bring water to a boil. Cut unpeeled eggplant into 1½-inch cubes. Drop into boiling water and boil for 5 to 10 minutes until soft but still solid. Drain eggplant in a colander, drop on paper towels and pat dry. Add the eggplant to the marinade in bowl and toss gently with a wooden spoon. Cover bowl and refrigerate for 1 to 2 hours.

When ready to serve, add olive oil and capers and toss gently with wooden spoon. Serve in a bowl with toothpicks as a snack before dinner or on individual plates on a bed of lettuce as a salad. Garnish with sprouts or watercress.

Serves 6-8 as a snack or 4 as a salad.

Zucchini Salad

Be adventurous with this unusual salad. When you're tired of lettuce, turn to the zucchini for a delicious change of salad pace. A perfect beginning for the Oxtail Stew in this section.

- 6 medium zucchini
- ¼ cup tarragon vinegar
- ½ teaspoon salt
- pepper to taste

- ¾ cup olive oil
- 2 shallots, minced
- 2 tablespoons chopped parsley
- 2 anchovies, mashed

Wash and scrub zucchini and drop whole into boiling water. Boil uncovered for about 5 minutes or until tender but firm. Drain and run cold water over zucchini. Cut off ends and slice in ¼-inch slices into a large bowl.

Combine remaining ingredients to make dressing. Pour dressing over zucchini and marinate in refrigerator for 1 hour, tossing occasionally. Serve on a bed of lettuce.

Serves 8

Pan Au Chocolat

The idea of serving a yeast bread stuffed with chocolate is a novel one. Be sure to serve these piping hot!

- 2½ cups all-purpose flour
- 4 tablespoons sugar
- 2 teaspoons salt
- 4 tablespoons butter
- 2 eggs
- 4 tablespoons sour cream
- 1 teaspoon grated lemon rind
- 1 package dry yeast
- 2 tablespoons lukewarm milk
- ¼ cup melted butter
- 2 4-ounce semi-sweet chocolate bars

In a large mixing bowl combine flour, sugar and salt. Add butter and mix until crumbly. Add egg, sour cream and lemon rind. In a cup combine yeast with lukewarm milk and add to the flour mixture beating until thoroughly blended. Lightly grease top of dough, cover with kitchen towel and let rise in a warm place for 2 hours or until double in bulk. Punch down and roll out on a lightly floured board ¼-inch thick. Cut into 3 inch squares. Brush each square with melted butter.

Cut chocolate bars into 1½ inch by ½ inch pieces and place in center of each square. Fold one side over chocolate, fold both ends over and cover with remaining end. Pinch with floured fingertips to seal and place sealed side down on buttered cookie sheet. Brush with melted butter, let butter harden for a few seconds, cover with kitchen towel and let rise for 45 minutes or until double in bulk.

Bake in preheated 375° oven for 20 minutes or until golden. Serve hot or remove to a wire rack to cool. Store in plastic bags in freezer. Defrost as needed and reheat in 375° oven as these are specially good when the chocolate inside is hot and melted.

Yields 2 to 3 dozen

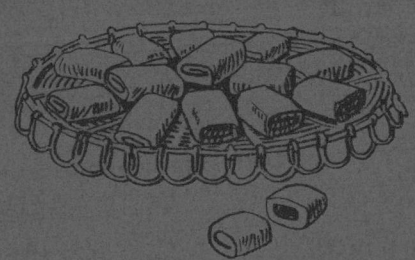

Tomato Stuffed Cheese Souffle

When you carry a platter of these gorgeous souffles out to the table, your guests will know why they may have had to wait. Because remember, people wait for souffles—souffles don't wait for people.

- 2 tablespoons butter
- 2 tablespoons all-purpose flour
- 1 cup milk
- 3 egg yolks
- 1 cup grated American cheese
- ¼ teaspoon dry mustard
- salt and pepper to taste
- 3 egg whites
- 10 medium-sized tomatoes

Melt butter in saucepan, add flour, stirring constantly until bubbling. Add half of milk and mix with wooden spoon. Add the remaining milk and cook, stirring until smooth and thick. Add some of hot milk mixture to yolks and then slowly pour yolk mixture into cream sauce. Add the cheese, dry mustard and salt and pepper. Pour into a bowl and cool.

Beat egg whites until stiff (but not dry) and fold into cheese mixture very gently but thoroughly. Cut tops off tomatoes about half an inch down and carefully scoop out pulp and seeds. Fill tomato shells with cheese mixture and place on a cookie sheet. Bake in preheated 350° oven for 50 minutes or until a rich golden brown. Serve immediately.

Serves 10

Spinach and Yogurt

Spinach and yogurt—what a combination! Layered and flavored with the spices of the Middle East, it will go well with most meat dishes.

- 3 bunches fresh spinach (or 2 10-ounce boxes frozen spinach)
- ¼ teaspoon allspice
- 2 tablespoons margarine
- 3 medium onions, chopped
- ¼ teaspoon salt
- ½ pound ground beef
- 1 8-ounce carton yogurt

Thoroughly wash spinach and remove any tough stems. Cook spinach until just tender, about 7-10 minutes. Drain off water and squeeze out any excess water. Place spinach in a glass baking pan and score into 2-inch squares. Sprinkle half of the allspice on the spinach. In a skillet, heat margarine and saute onions until soft. Spoon onions on spinach evenly. Pour the salt onto the skillet. When hot, add meat and brown, stirring to crumble. Add remaining allspice. Evenly spread meat onto onions. Top with a layer of yogurt and place in a preheated 375° oven for 2 or 3 minutes, or until yogurt is heated. Garnish with strips of pimiento.

Serves 4-6

Cantonese Fried Rice

It's not so inscrutable as it seems. You can make fried rice just as good as any Chinese restaurant. To easily assemble this recipe, have all ingredients pre-measured.

- 3 tablespoons vegetable oil
- ¼ teaspoon salt
- 1 egg
- ¼ cup diced chicken, pork or bacon
- ¼ cup bean sprouts, chopped
- 3 cups cooked rice (cooled)
- 2 teaspoons soy sauce
- dash of pepper
- ¼ cup green onions, chopped

Heat vegetable oil in a skillet and add salt. Scramble egg, add chicken, bean sprouts and rice, and mix. Fry well on low heat, add soy sauce, pepper and green onions and mix well. Can be reheated on low heat.

Serves 6

Rolled Sole with Muscat and Grapes

This is a variation of the theme—Sole Veronique. Note the sweet wine, rather than dry, and the fish is stuffed and rolled, rather than flat.

- 1 medium onion, chopped
- 2 tomatoes, chopped
- 1 green pepper, chopped
- 2 garlic cloves, minced
- 12 pieces fillet of sole (or any flounder)
- salt and pepper
- 2 tablespoons parsley
- 1 teaspoon marjoram
- 1 teaspoon thyme
- 1 teaspoon tarragon
- ¼ cup butter or margarine
- 1 bunch grapes, seedless white (canned optional—drained)
- muscat wine

In a small bowl, mix together the onion, tomatoes, green pepper, and garlic. Place fillets on waxed paper smooth-side down and spread on equal amounts of tomato mixture. Combine herbs and sprinkle half the amount on each fillet. Roll the fillets, starting at small end and place in a shallow glass baking dish, seam side down. Dot with butter and sprinkle with reserved herb mixture. Add grapes and wine and bake in preheated 375° oven for 15 to 20 minutes. Baste to keep fish moist.

Serves 6

Shrimp Tempura

A whole dinner can be made tempura-style by dipping chunks of raw vegetables in this batter and deep frying until golden brown.

- 1½ pounds shrimp (16-20 to the pound)
- 1 egg
- 1 cup water
- 1 teaspoon vegetable oil
- 2 tablespoons cornstarch
- 1 cup all-purpose flour
- 1 teaspoon salt
- oil for frying

Shell and clean shrimp leaving tail on, split through back cutting almost through. Beat egg with water and vegetable oil. Combine cornstarch, flour and salt. Add to egg mixture and beat well for batter. Heat oil to 375°. Dip shrimp through batter holding tail and drop gently into oil. When shrimp rise to surface, turn and continue cooking until golden brown. Drain on paper towels and serve immediately with shrimp sauce or Chinese mustard.

Serves 6

Chow Yuk

A Disneyland stand-by, this versatile Chinese main dish can be made with veal, beef, chicken or pork. Improvise with other vegetables that you have on hand to create your own version.

- 4 tablespoons vegetable oil
- 2 pounds fresh turkey breast, sliced
- 1½ teaspoons salt
- 2 onions, sliced
- 1½ cups celery, sliced
- ½ pound fresh mushrooms, sliced
- 1 8-ounce can bamboo shoots, sliced
- 1 8-ounce can water chestnuts, sliced
- 1 10½-ounce can chicken broth
- 4 ounces fresh Chinese peas (or 1 6-ounce package frozen)
- 1 tablespoon cornstarch
- 2 tablespoons cold water

Heat oil in a skillet and brown turkey breast slices, seasoned with salt. Add onions, celery, mushrooms, bamboo shoots and water chestnuts and saute together. Stir in chicken broth and Chinese peas and simmer until peas are tender. Combine cornstarch and water and make a paste. Gradually add cornstarch paste to skillet stirring constantly. Bring to a boil. Serve with steamed rice or Cantonese Fried Rice found in this section.

Serves 6-8

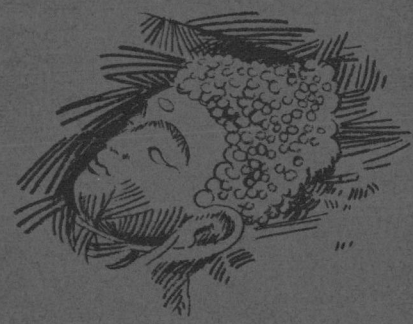

Cornish Game Hens with Garlic Lemon Sauce

Talk about an adventure, this recipe calls for one whole unpeeled garlic bud. It flavors both the hens and the sauce fantastically! By the way, freeze these unused egg whites and use them later in our Schaum Torte recipe found in this section.

- 2 12-ounce Cornish game hens
- 1 whole garlic bud, unpeeled and halved
- 6 tablespoons margarine
- 4 egg yolks
- ¾ cup heavy cream
- juice of 1 lemon
- ¼ cup butter
- ¼ cup all-purpose flour
- 1 cup chicken stock
- ½ teaspoon salt

Fill cavity of each hen with half of the garlic and 2 tablespoons margarine. Tie wings and legs with string to keep together. Rub outside of hens with remaining margarine, salt and pepper, and roast on a rack, breast down, over foil-lined pan in preheated 375-400° oven for 35 minutes. Untie string and remove garlic and continue roasting hens an additional 15 minutes or until tender.

While the hens are roasting, peel and press cooked garlic through a garlic press into a small bowl and beat in egg yolks, cream and lemon juice and set aside. In a saucepan, melt butter and stir in flour; cook over low heat, stirring for 3 minutes. Gradually add chicken stock, stirring constantly and simmer the sauce over moderate heat for 5 to 10 minutes. Remove the pan from the heat and strain garlic mixture into chicken mixture, beating with a wire whisk. Return to low heat and mix until sauce thickens.

Cut each hen in half lengthwise and place on individual plates. Spoon sauce over hens and serve remaining sauce on the side. Leftover sauce can be frozen.

Serves 4

Oxtail Stew

Here's an exciting old-country recipe that is economical and savory. Boil some noodles, spoon on this stew, and you'll enjoy every drop of this rich gravy.

- ⅓ cup vegetable oil
- 2 medium onions, sliced
- 3 cloves garlic, chopped
- 4 to 5 pounds oxtails
- 2 teaspoons salt
- ½ teaspoon pepper
- ½ cup all-purpose flour
- 5 carrots, peeled & sliced
- 1 parsnip, peeled & sliced
- 2 celery stalks, sliced
- 1 cup red wine
- 2 cups chicken or beef stock
- 1 tablespoon tomato paste
- ½ teaspoon thyme, crushed
- 4 whole cloves
- 1 bay leaf
- 3 tablespoons parsley, chopped
- ½ cup Madeira (optional)
- ½ pound fresh mushrooms, halved (optional)

In a Dutch oven, heat oil and saute onions and garlic until soft. Remove onions and garlic with slotted spoon and set aside on a large plate. While onions are sauteing, season oxtails with salt and pepper, roll in flour, shaking off any excess flour. Place oxtails in Dutch oven, in one layer. Turn oxtails, browning on all sides. Remove to large plate and continue browning oxtails until all are done. Return onions, garlic and oxtails to the Dutch oven and add all remaining ingredients except Madeira and mushrooms, mixing thoroughly. Bring to a boil, stirring occasionally to avoid sticking. Cover the Dutch oven and place in a preheated 325° oven and bake for 3 hours. Add Madeira and mushrooms and bake, uncovered, for one additional hour or until oxtails are tender. Before serving, skim off excess grease. (This stew can be prepared in advance and refrigerated. Grease will congeal and will be easy to remove. Reheat in a 325° oven for 45 minutes before serving.)

Serves 8-10

Marinated Pork Chops

The mustard-anchovy paste, so easy to prepare, is a taste delight not only on the pork chops suggested here but also on lamb chops, steaks, veal chops or even hamburger.

Marinade:
- ¼ cup oil
- 1 clove garlic, chopped fine
- ½ teaspoon oregano, crushed
- ⅛ teaspoon pepper
- 8 pork chops, wafer thin

Combine all ingredients except pork chops. Place chops in one layer in a glass baking dish. Pour marinade over chops and let sit for 4 hours.

Mustard paste:
- 2 tablespoons Dijon mustard
- 1 tablespoon anchovy paste
- juice of ½ a lemon
- 1 teaspoon oregano, crushed
- 1 clove garlic, chopped fine

Combine all ingredients and mix well.

Remove chops from marinade and spread one side with half the mustard paste. Broil or charcoal broil, coated side up, for 3 or 4 minutes. Turn and spread uncooked side with remaining mustard paste. Broil an additional 4 minutes. Sprinkle with parsley and serve at once.

Serves 4

Far East Stuffed Figs

Truly this is a "finger food"... made with the fingers and eaten with the fingers. To be served with an after-dinner beverage.

- ½ cup whole blanched almonds
- 18 large figs, dried
- 3 tablespoons semisweet chocolate, finely grated

Place almonds on a foil-lined baking sheet and toast them in a preheated 350° oven for 5 to 10 minutes until lightly golden, just before they crack. Reserve 18 whole almonds and blend the remaining very fine. Grate or blend the chocolate and combine with the grated almonds.

With a sharp knife or kitchen scissors cut stems off figs. With your finger, make a depression inside each fig pushing the pulp to the sides and smoothing it out to make room for the filling. Fill inside of each fig with chocolate-almond mixture. Pinch the opening to seal. Stand the figs upright on an ungreased baking sheet and bake in a preheated 350° oven for 5 to 10 minutes. Turn the figs over and bake another 5 to 10 minutes, being careful not to burn bottom.

Remove baking sheet from oven. Stuff each fig with the reserved whole toasted almond and reseal. Serve hot or cold.

Yields 18

Schaum Torte

Super rich, super light, super sweet ... it's really super! It's important to remember to fill the meringue shells at the very last second to preserve crispness.

Meringue:
- 3 egg whites
- 1 cup sugar
- 1 tablespoon vinegar
- 1 teaspoon vanilla

Chantilly:
- 1 pint whipping cream
- 2 tablespoons confectioners sugar
- ½ teaspoon vanilla
- ½ teaspoon orange liqueur (optional)
- 1 large can crushed pineapple
- 4 bananas

Beat egg whites until stiff. Add sugar, vinegar and vanilla and beat into a light meringue. Pour into greased muffin tins, ⅔ full. Bake in preheated 250° oven for 1 hour. Carefully loosen sides with a knife and remove from tins. Place on cookie sheet to cool. Can hold at this point for several hours before filling.

Whip cream until soft peaks are formed, add 2 tablespoons confectioners sugar and ½ teaspoon vanilla or orange liqueur. Refrigerate.

Drain liquid from pineapple. Slice banana into quarters lengthwise and then into thin slices. Mix with pineapple. Refrigerate.

Cut off top of meringue very gently. Set top aside. Alternate a scoop of chantilly and a spoonful of fruit twice and top with lid of meringue. Top with a teaspoonful of chantilly and a dab of fruit. Serve at once.

Serves 9

TOMORROWLAND

TOMORROWLAND—a new world on the move—lets you participate today in adventures which are a living blueprint of our future. Unknown when Disneyland was born in 1955, technological terms like lasers, fly-bys, astronauts and communications satellites are familiar here and now. You can rocket to another planet in Disneyland's *Mission to Mars,* dive to the depths of the sea in the *Submarine Voyage,* preview tomorrow's mass transit on the Disneyland-Alweg Monorail System, and drive real "sports cars" over the fastest super highway in the world—*Autopia.* And with these modern recipes, you can enjoy menus of tomorrow—today.

Astronaut's Cold Cucumber Soup

A little bit on the tangy side, this unusual cold soup is refreshingly good all year round. The ease of blender cooking makes this recipe a snap.

- 4 cucumbers, sliced
- 3 cups chicken stock
- 1 pint sour cream
- 2 tablespoons vinegar
- 2 cloves garlic, chopped
- 1½ teaspoons salt
- ½ teaspoon dill weed

Place cucumbers and 1 cup chicken stock in blender and blend. Add sour cream, vinegar, garlic and blend thoroughly. Pour into a large bowl, add the rest of the chicken stock, salt and dill weed and mix well. Refrigerate. Garnish with minced parsley and unpeeled chopped cucumber or a dollop of sour cream and dill weed.

Serves 6

Asparagus Soup

Madeira or sherry brings out subtle flavors from asparagus that you would never suspect, especially in a soup. Pop-Up Bread, found in the Main Street section, is the ideal accompaniment.

- 3 pounds asparagus
- 3 cups chicken stock
- 3 tablespoons butter
- 1/3 cup onions, chopped
- 1/2 cup parsley, chopped
- 1 tablespoon all-purpose flour
- 1/2 cup heavy cream
- 2 tablespoons lemon juice
- 1 teaspoon salt
- 1/8 teaspoon white pepper
- 1/2 cup Madeira or sherry

Cook asparagus in chicken stock until tender. Cut one inch off tops of asparagus and reserve. In a large saucepan heat butter, add onions and parsley, and saute until soft. Add flour and cook over low heat, stirring constantly with a wooden spoon for 2 or 3 minutes. Stir in the chicken stock with asparagus, cover and simmer 5 additional minutes. Puree in blender in small portions and return to saucepan. Add cream and cook over low heat until hot, but not boiling. Add lemon juice, salt and pepper to taste. Add wine and simmer 5 more minutes. Serve hot, garnished with reserved asparagus tips.

Serves 6-8

Chicken Liver Paté

As blender patés go, this new one must rank near the top as the easiest and most flavorful of them all. The cognac here not only releases the flavors of the ingredients, but also acts as a preservative.

- 2 pounds chicken livers, uncooked
- 3 eggs
- ⅓ cup cognac
- 1½ cups mocha mix or cream

- ⅔ cups fresh chicken fat
- 1 onion, coarsely chopped
- ½ cup all-purpose flour

- 5 teaspoons salt
- 1 teaspoon ground ginger
- 1 teaspoon Accent
- 2 teaspoons white pepper
- 1 teaspoon allspice

In a blender, blend livers, eggs, cognac and cream. Add chicken fat, onion and flour and blend thoroughly. Add remaining ingredients and blend.

Pour into greased mold or loaf pan and cover with double thickness foil. Place in a pan of water in preheated 325° oven and bake 2½ hours. Remove foil, cool and invert onto a plate and garnish with parsley. Decorate with capers, pimientos, cucumbers or sliced Dill Pickles (recipe in Main Street section).

Served with toasted rye bread (recipe in this section) or crackers.

Natural Health Food Salad

Everything in this salad is good for you and tastes good too. The sweet-and-sour dressing enlivens the natural ingredients. It goes with everything, and everybody goes for it.

Salad Dressing:
- 4 tablespoons vegetable oil
- juice of 2 lemons
- ⅓ cup honey
- ½ teaspoon salt
- ¼ teaspoon pepper
- 2 teaspoons poppy seeds
- ¼ teaspoon celery seeds
- 1 teaspoon red wine vinegar
- 3 red apples, cored, cut in eighths and sliced thin

Combine all ingredients except apples and blend thoroughly. Add apples and set aside until ready to use.

Salad:
- 1 medium jicama, peeled and sliced julienne
- 1 medium cucumber, quartered lengthwise and sliced thin
- 1 cup cashews, coarsely chopped
- ½ pound bean sprouts

In a large salad bowl, combine all ingredients and refrigerate until ready to serve. When ready to serve, pour in dressing and toss salad, spreading dressing evenly.

Serves 8

Tabbouleh Salad
(CRACKED WHEAT)

A new taste treat, and rapidly gaining popularity, is the centuries-old crushed wheat salad from the Middle East. Use this instead of potato salad.

- 2 cups crushed wheat (burghul wheat)
- 1 cup parsley, chopped fine
- ½ cup onions, chopped
- 3 tablespoons scallions, sliced
- 3 tomatoes, chopped
- 1 cup lemon juice
- 1 cup vegetable oil
- ½ teaspoon salt
- ¼ teaspoon pepper
- 1 tablespoon fresh mint, chopped (optional)

Cover burghul wheat with boiling water and let stand for 2 to 3 hours. Drain and press out any excess water with back of a spoon. Toss the wheat lightly with remaining ingredients. Chill until ready to serve. Serve on a bed of red lettuce and garnish with lemon slices.

Serves 12

Stuffed Pear Shells

Everybody has tasted applesauce, but who has tasted (much less made) pear sauce? It's a wonder why not, because it's so easy to do and delicious to taste. Could also serve as a dessert, along with a platter of assorted cheeses.

- 8 pears
- 2 tablespoons lemon juice

Peel, core and slice 4 of the pears. Place in a saucepan and sprinkle with lemon juice. Set aside.

Cut top off the 4 remaining pears and with a grapefruit spoon, remove the pulp ⅛-inch from skin. Add the pulp to the saucepan discarding seeds and core. Place pear shells on serving plate. Using a paring knife, cut small V's around top edge to create a scalloped edge. Sprinkle pear shells with lemon juice to prevent browning. Cover with plastic wrap and refrigerate.

Cook pear slices and pulp in saucepan on very low fire until tender. Put in a blender and blend, leaving pear sauce as coarse as desired. Cool. (If sweeter pear sauce is desired, you can add sugar or artificial sweetener to taste.)

Spoon cooled sauce into pear shells and refrigerate until ready to serve.

Garnish top with sprig of parsley or mint leaf. Good accompaniment to main dish, such as meat or chicken.

Serves 4

One-Step Rye Bread or Rolls

The beauty of this simple recipe is that you no longer have to be intimidated when baking with yeast. This dough rises but once and is ready for baking.

- 2½ cups milk
- 3 tablespoons shortening
- 3 tablespoons brown sugar
- 1 tablespoon salt
- 2 tablespoons caraway seeds
- 2 packages dry yeast
- ½ cup lukewarm water
- ½ teaspoon sugar
- 8 cups rye flour
- 3 tablespoons vegetable oil
- 3 tablespoons yellow corn meal
- 1 egg, beaten

In a saucepan, heat milk to the scalding point. Pour scalded milk into a large mixing bowl and add shortening, brown sugar, salt and caraway seeds. Mix to dissolve shortening and cool to lukewarm.

Dissolve yeast in lukewarm water with sugar and add to lukewarm milk mixture. Mix thoroughly. Continue mixing, adding rye flour, one cup at a time until dough is stiff enough to knead by hand. Turn out onto a floured board and knead, adding enough flour (if necessary) to make a soft dough. Overkneading is not good for this bread.

Divide dough into 3 parts. Each part can be rolled into a round or oval loaf or can be made into 12 small round or oval rolls. Oil a cookie sheet and sprinkle it with corn meal. Place loaves or rolls on cookie sheet, cover with kitchen towel and let rise in a warm place about 30 minutes or just before top begins to crack. Brush with beaten egg and sprinkle with caraway seeds.

Bake in a pre-heated 375° oven for 30 minutes or until top begins to brown. Cool bread on a wire rack. When completely cool, bread can be stored in plastic bags in freezer and defrosted when needed. If frozen, warm in a 350° oven before serving.

Yields: 3 loaves, or 36 to 45 rolls.

Broccoli with Almonds, Onions and Garlic

This is a garlic-lovers delight that should appeal to everyone. For the more timid, start with only two cloves of garlic. You'll graduate to four or more cloves fast when you learn to appreciate its pungent flavor. The trick in keeping broccoli green is to plunge it into boiling water, cook until just tender and then immediately refresh it under cold water, which stops the cooking action.

- 2 pounds fresh broccoli
- ½ teaspoon salt

- ⅓ cup olive oil or margarine
- ⅓ cup blanched almonds, sliced

- 2-4 cloves garlic, minced
- ½ medium onion, chopped
- 3 tablespoons capers (optional), drained and chopped
- salt and pepper to taste

Remove and separate flowerets from broccoli and peel stems. Half lengthwise and cut into 1½-inch pieces. Add ½ teaspoon salt to boiling water and drop broccoli in. Boil for 4-5 minutes. Drain water and refresh under cold water and drain. Set aside on paper towels.

Heat oil in a large skillet, add almonds and saute until brown. Add garlic and cook until just brown and remove with slotted spoon. Set aside. Saute onion in skillet until just brown and combine with garlic. Add broccoli to skillet and toss gently over moderate heat for 2 minutes. Add ½ cup water and cook broccoli, covered, for 6 minutes or until tender. Add almonds, garlic, onions, capers and salt and pepper and cook uncovered over high heat for 1 minute, stirring with a wooden spoon. Serve immediately.

Serves 6-8

Versatile Blender Sauce for Vegetables

There's little chance of curdling or separating when you follow this modern blender method of preparing this bearnaise-type sauce. A convenience tip is to store the prepared hot sauce in a thermos, which has been rinsed with hot water. The sauce is then ready to pour hours later when you need it.

- ¼ pound butter
- 3 egg yolks
- ½ teaspoon salt
- 1 teaspoon tarragon
- 1 tablespoon chopped onion
- 2 tablespoons wine vinegar

Heat butter until bubbly. Combine remaining ingredients in blender and blend on low speed for 5 seconds. Turn blender to high speed and pour in butter in steady stream into egg mixture. When thick and yellow, transfer to double boiler and keep hot, but not boiling.

Yields 1 cup

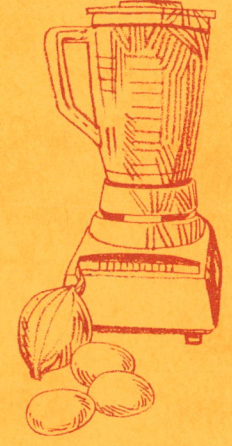

Onion Crepes with Sour Cream and Caviar

No, it's not as expensive as it sounds. Domestic caviar is just as tasty in this first dish and costs a fraction as much as imports. The unusual feature here is the use of onion in the crepe batter. For an interesting variety, replace the caviar with slices of Gravlax, found in the Fantasyland section.

- 1¼ cups all-purpose flour
- 1 tablespoon sugar
- ¼ teaspoon salt
- 3 eggs
- 2 cups milk
- ½ cup onions, chopped fine
- 1 tablespoon butter
- 1 tablespoon orange liqueur or cognac
- 1 pint sour cream
- 3 1½-ounce jars black lumpfish caviar
- ¼ cup scallions, sliced thin

Sift flour, sugar and salt into a large mixing bowl. In a small bowl, beat together the eggs and milk and add to the flour mixture and mix until thoroughly blended. Add onions and mix well. Stir in melted butter and orange liqueur or cognac. Cover and let stand for 1½ to 2 hours.

Stir batter from bottom and pour one heaping tablespoon into a buttered hot frying pan; swirl frying pan around gently, pouring out the excess batter into the bowl. This makes the crepe thinner. Should you wish to use a crepe pan, dip it into batter and cook according to regular method. Cook the crepe for about 1 or 2 minutes until it starts to brown. Drop onto a towel and then spread 4 at a time on a plate, cover with waxed paper and continue to layer them.

Across center of each crepe, spoon sour cream and caviar, and fold one side of the crepe then the other over filling. Place a dollop of sour cream, a dab of caviar and a sprinkle of scallions on top.

Yields 2 dozen and Serves 12

Cold Poached Salmon

Polish up your best platter for this stunning fish dish. Don't broil or bake this salmon, poach it to more fully appreciate how moist and flavorful it can be.

- 1 onion, sliced
- 2 stalks celery
- 2 carrots, cut in chunks or sliced
- 3 sprigs parsley
- 1 pound fish for chowder
- 1-2 cups dry white wine
- 1 teaspoon salt
- ¼ teaspoon pepper
- 1 6-pound whole salmon

On the bottom of a fish poacher or long roaster pan place onions, celery, carrots, parsley, fish for chowder, wine and salt and pepper. Bring to a boil, cover and simmer for 20 minutes.

Have fish market man remove center bone from salmon. Place salmon on rack of poacher or wrap salmon with cheesecloth tied on ends, leaving cheesecloth dangling for easy handling or lifting. Poach for 30 minutes or until just tender to touch and skin becomes soft. Remove fish carefully to a large platter and cool. Carefully peel off skin, cover with saran wrap and refrigerate until ready to cover with sauce.

Garnish:
- 1 cup Green Mayonnaise Sauce (recipe in Fantasyland)
- 1 large cucumber, sliced thin

Spread green mayonnaise over salmon evenly and arrange cucumbers, overlapping, to resemble fish scales.

Serves 8-10

Rabbit Provençal

Now's the time to be really adventurous ... try rabbit in place of chicken! Millions of Europeans love it, and have for centuries, and you'll know why when you try this new taste experience.

- 1 rabbit (about 3 pounds)
- 2 slices bacon
- 4 tablespoons vegetable oil
- 1 onion, chopped
- 1 clove garlic, minced
- ½ green pepper, chunked
- 1 32-ounce can tomatoes (drained) or 8 peeled fresh tomatoes
- 1 tablespoon tomato paste
- 1 teaspoon salt
- 8 peppercorns or ½ teaspoon ground pepper
- 2 cups red wine
- 2 bouillon cubes, diluted in ½ cup water
- 1 teaspoon tarragon

Cut rabbit into serving pieces. Saute small pieces of sliced bacon in hot oil. Add onions, garlic, green pepper, tomatoes and rabbit. Cover with red wine. Simmer 1½ hours or until rabbit is tender. Remove rabbit to a serving bowl and cook sauce down. Pour sauce over rabbit and serve.

Serves 4

Note: This recipe can be used and cooked in a crockpot with cooking time 12-14 hours on low heat setting.

Tomorrowland Turkey Kabobs

Up until recently, most people only thought of preparing turkey roasted whole. Now, in modern supermarkets, turkey parts are readily available for a variety of dishes. Kabob your turkey for a tasty change.

- 1 turkey breast or 5 chicken breasts
- ½ cup soy sauce
- ½ cup sherry
- 1 teaspoon brown sugar
- ¼ teaspoon ginger powder
- 20 small mushrooms
- 1 red bell pepper, cut in squares

Cut boned turkey or chicken breasts into 1 inch cubes, making about 20 cubes. Combine soy sauce, sherry, sugar and ginger in a saucepan and bring to a boil. Simmer until reduced about one quarter. Cool and add turkey. Marinate at least one hour. Using bamboo skewers which have been soaked in water to prevent burning, thread a turkey cube, a mushroom, a piece of pepper and a mushroom and a turkey cube. Continue until all ingredients are on remaining skewers. Just before grilling or broiling, brush each kabob with marinade and cook until lightly browned, turning once, or about 5 minutes on each side.

Serves 10

Sweet and Sour Meatballs

The long, slow cooking in the modern electric crockpot develops all these flavors to their fullest. Great for a buffet, the crockpot is practical when you cook in it and pretty when you serve from it.

- 1 pound veal, ground
- 1 pound beef, ground
- 3 cloves garlic
- 2 onions, chopped fine
- 1/3 cup vegetable oil
- 2 eggs
- 1/2 cup parsley, minced
- 1 teaspoon salt
- 1/2 teaspoon pepper
- 1/4 cup bread crumbs
- 2 cups beef stock
- 1/4 cup sugar
- 1 tablespoon vinegar or lemon juice
- 2 tablespoons tomato paste

In a large mixing bowl mix veal and beef together. Set aside. In a saucepan, saute garlic and onion in 3 tablespoons of oil until soft. Work this into the meat mixture. Add eggs, parsley, salt and pepper. Mix in bread crumbs thoroughly. Shape into 4 dozen meatballs. Add remaining oil to the saucepan and brown meatballs.

In an electric crockery cooker, combine beef stock, sugar, vinegar and tomato paste and add meatballs. Cook on low heat for 3-4 hours. Serve as appetizers or as main course over rice.

Yields 4 dozen

Apricot Sorbet with Chocolate Garni

Just listen for the "ooh" and "aahs" when you bring out a tray of these impressive sherbet desserts. Fun to make, it's an all-weather, all-occasion dessert.

- 1 28-ounce can apricots
- 1 cup sugar
- ½ cup wine (sweet muscat or sherry)
- ¼ cup lemon juice
- 1 pint cream, whipped (reserve 1 cup for garnish)

Drain apricots, reserve juice in large bowl and remove seeds. Place apricots in blender and blend (don't puree). Return to juice and add sugar, wine and lemon juice and mix well. Freeze to a soft mush. Fold in whipped cream and freeze 1½ hours. Spoon into wine glasses or sherbet cups. Top with reserved whipped cream which has been flavored with 2 teaspoons muscat and sweetened with powdered sugar. Place a chocolate garni in each serving.

CHOCOLATE GARNI:
- 1 12-ounce package chocolate chips

In a double boiler over simmering water, melt chocolate chips. Stir and let cool. Pour into a pastry bag with a star tip. Place a sheet of wax paper on a cookie sheet and make 4-inch candy cane shapes of the chocolate. Refrigerate until chocolate is firm and peels easily off wax paper. Keep in refrigerator until ready to serve.

Yields 12

Quick Blender Chocolate Mousse

Short and sweet, this has to be the quickest and easiest-to-make dessert ever. The coffee flavors blend beautifully with the chocolate.

- 1½ cups chocolate chips
- 3 eggs
- 4½ tablespoons liquid coffee
- 3 tablespoons Kahlua
- 1⅛ cups scalded milk

Combine all of the above ingredients in blender. Blend at high speed for 2 minutes. Pour into wine glasses and chill.
Serves 4

NEW ORLEANS SQUARE

NEW ORLEANS SQUARE — A Dixie-like delight — dramatically recreates the exciting legend of the Crescent City way back in 1850. Let your mind drift back to this golden age as you walk along its narrow, winding streets and in sheltered courtyards and relive the days when she was the "Gay Paree" of the American frontier. Here you'll find Disneyland's most distinctive adventures in shopping and dining. And here also, *"The Pirates of the Caribbean"* adventure recreates the buccaneering past of the Spanish Main. In *New Orleans Square,* you'll discover creative Creole and Southern cooking that will season up your fancy get-togethers and add a culinary dash of spice to your everyday life.

Shrimp and Oyster Gumbo

A real meal in a bowl, this sausage-added revision of an old standby uses both okra and gumbo filé to give it more body rather than one or the other as most recipes call for. Don't be shy to dip pieces of garlic toast to get the very last drops of gumbo.

- ½ cup vegetable oil
- ½ cup all-purpose flour
- 1 pound smoked sausage (Polish or French), sliced
- 2 pounds fresh shrimp, peeled and deveined

- 2 tablespoons vegetable oil
- 2 cups onions, chopped
- 30 pods fresh okra, sliced ½ inch thick (canned okra can be substituted)
- 3 cloves garlic, chopped fine
- ⅔ cup green peppers, chopped
- ½ cup scallions, sliced thin
- 2 tablespoons parsley, chopped
- 1 teaspoon salt
- 4 13½-ounce cans chicken stock
- 4 16-ounce cans tomatoes, cut in chunks
- ½ pound oysters
- 2 tablespoons filé powder

Combine oil and flour in a saucepan and heat, stirring constantly until milk chocolate in color. Add sausage and cook for 5 minutes. Add shrimp and cook an additional 5 minutes and set aside.

Heat oil in large pot, add onions and okra and cook until soft. Add garlic, green pepper, scallions, parsley and salt and cook 5 minutes. Add chicken stock and tomatoes, including liquid. Simmer, covered, for 45 minutes. Add oysters and continue cooking for 5 minutes. Remove from heat and add filé powder. Let gumbo stand for 5 minutes before serving, stirring occasionally. Serve in deep bowls plain or over steamed rice, with thick slices of French bread.

Serves 8-10

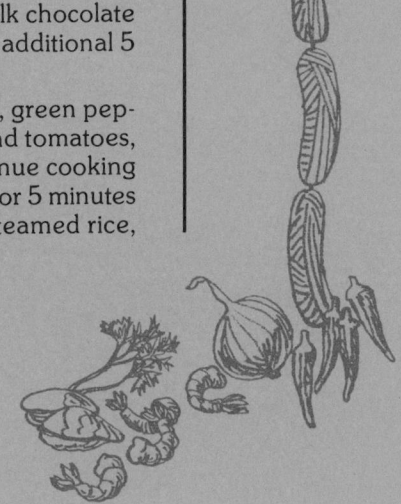

French Market Onion Soup

This French-style onion soup is enhanced with the enrichment of the beef stock with vegetables. Easy to make, always a favorite.

- 3 pints water
- 2½ ounces beef bouillon
- 4 carrots, peeled and sliced
- 2 celery stalks, with tops
- 1 parsnip, peeled and sliced
- 3 sprigs parsley, chopped

- ½ cup butter, unsalted
- 3 large onions, sliced thin (4 cups)
- 1 teaspoon sugar

- ¼ pint brandy (optional)
- 1 teaspoon salt
- ¼ teaspoon pepper
- 4 slices French bread, toasted
- 1 cup gruyere cheese grated (or use Swiss cheese)
- 2 tablespoons parsley, chopped, for garnish

In a saucepan, bring water and bouillon to a boil, add carrots, celery, parsnip and parsley. Simmer for 15 minutes. Strain and set aside.

In a large skillet, heat butter, add onions and sugar and cook them very gently over a low heat, stirring occasionally until the onions are golden brown (about 30 to 45 minutes). Gradually add the strained beef stock and blend with onions. Bring the soup to a boil, lower the heat, cover and simmer gently for 1 hour. Just before serving, stir in the brandy and salt and pepper to taste. Place six ovenproof cups and saucers on a cookie sheet, ladle in soup and top with toast. Sprinkle generously with cheese and place in preheated 400° oven. Bake until the cheese is melted and golden brown.

Serves 4

Br'er Bear's Okra Salad

Not usually found outside New Orleans, this Cajun Okra Salad is an unusually tasty way to enjoy this uncommon vegetable.

- 1 cup okra, sliced and cooked (or 9 ounces frozen, cooked)
- 2 tomatoes, quartered
- 1 teaspoon lemon juice
- ½ teaspoon chili powder
- ½ teaspoon salt
- ¼ teaspoon white pepper
- 1 teaspoon parsley, chopped
- lettuce
- 1 hard-boiled egg, grated

Combine okra and tomatoes in large bowl. Chill. Toss with lemon juice, salt, chili powder, pepper and parsley. Serve on a bed of lettuce. Garnish with grated hard-cooked egg.
Serves 4

Rice and Mushrooms

Transform your ordinary entree into something very special by accompanying it with this side dish. Especially good with veal or lamb, or the Creole Chicken recipe elsewhere in this section.

- ½ cup sweet butter or margarine
- 1 cup mushrooms, fresh preferred
- ½ teaspoon salt
- ⅛ teaspoon pepper
- 2 cups rice, cooked (substitute chicken stock for water when preparing rice)

Heat butter in large skillet. Slice mushrooms and add to butter. Add salt and pepper and saute until mushrooms are soft. Set aside until ready to serve. Add rice and saute for 12 minutes.
Serves 4

Sweet Potato Souffle

The simple secret to a successful souffle is the proper handling of the egg whites. Use a light hand when folding in the egg whites and you'll end up with a light souffle.

- 3 cups sweet potatoes, cooked and mashed (fresh or canned)
- ⅓ cup medium dry sherry
- 1¼ cups half-and-half
- 6 tablespoons butter or margarine, melted
- 3 teaspoons orange peel, grated
- 1 teaspoon salt
- ⅛ teaspoon pepper
- ¼ teaspoon nutmeg
- ¼ teaspoon cinnamon
- 2 tablespoons brown sugar
- 6 eggs, separated

In a large mixing bowl, combine sweet potatoes, sherry, half-and-half, butter, orange peel, salt, pepper, nutmeg, cinnamon and sugar. Beat with electric mixer until blended. Add egg yolks and beat thoroughly. Set aside. Beat egg whites until stiff but moist, forming soft peaks, and gently fold into potato mixture. Butter a 2-quart souffle dish and pour in souffle mixture. Bake in preheated 375° oven for 45 minutes or until light brown on top.

Serves 10-12

Seafood Créole

Serve it tonight as a hot main dish, then follow up the next day as a cold salad on a bed of lettuce.

- ⅓ cup vegetable oil
- 1 cup green pepper, coarsely chopped
- 2 cups onion, coarsely chopped
- 1 cup celery, chopped
- 2 teaspoons garlic, minced
- 1 28-ounce can whole tomatoes
- ¼ teaspoon cayenne
- 1 tablespoon paprika
- 1 teaspoon salt
- 3 cups beef broth
- 1 bay leaf
- 2 pounds mixed raw seafood, such as shrimp, sea bass, crab and halibut
- 2 tablespoons cornstarch

Heat vegetable oil and saute green pepper, onion, celery and garlic until tender. Add remaining ingredients except seafood and cornstarch and simmer for 15 minutes. Add seafood and continue simmering 10 to 12 minutes more. If desired, thicken sauce with cornstarch mixed in a little cold water. Serve over hot fluffy rice.

Serves 8

Pompano En Parchment Paper

Here's a dramatic new version of an old New Orleans favorite. Open the paper wrapping right at the table to fully enjoy the escaping aroma.

- 1 pound fish trimmings
- 2 cups water
- 2 onions, sliced
- 1 bay leaf, crumbled
- 8 peppercorns, whole
- 1 teaspoon salt

- ½ cup butter
- 4 8-ounce pompano fillets (or sole, red snapper or flounder)

- ¼ cup scallions, chopped
- 2 tablespoons parsley, chopped
- 1 pound small shrimp, uncooked
- ½ cup dry white wine
- 1 tablespoon all-purpose flour
- 3 tablespoons cream
- ¼ teaspoon cayenne, ground

- parchment or wax paper

Combine 1-pound fish trimmings with water, onions, bay leaf, peppercorns and salt and bring to a boil and simmer for 30 minutes. Strain and set stock aside.

Butter a large baking dish using 2 tablespoons of butter. Place fillets in dish and spread with 1 tablespoon of butter and wax paper. Bake in preheated 350° oven for 5 minutes or until transparent. Transfer to a platter and set aside.

In a saucepan, melt 5 tablespoons butter, add scallions and parsley and saute until soft; add shrimp, wine, 1 cup stock and flour and cook until sauce thickens—about 5 minutes. Stir in cream and cayenne. Using 4 sheets of paper, 11" by 14", brush top with butter. Place 1 fillet of fish on half of each sheet of paper and top with shrimp sauce. Fold paper in half and crimp edges securely. Place on greased baking sheet and bake in preheated 450° oven for 10 minutes or until paper is golden brown. Serve at once in paper.

Serves 4

New Orleans Shrimp Etouffee

The fancy name "etouffee" is simply a method of cooking fish, meat or poultry smothered in a blanket of chopped vegetables. This robust, highly-spiced stew can be made well in advance and reheated, but don't overcook the second time around!

- 6 tablespoons butter or margarine
- ¼ cup all-purpose flour
- 1 cup onion, chopped
- ½ cup green pepper, chopped
- ½ cup celery, chopped
- 1 tablespoon garlic, minced
- 1 pound medium-size raw shrimp, peeled and deveined
- 1 teaspoon salt
- ¼ teaspoon pepper
- ¼ teaspoon cayenne
- juice of half a lemon
- ⅓ cup scallions, sliced
- 2 tablespoons parsley, chopped
- 1 cup cold water
- 2 cups hot water
- boiled rice

In a heavy 5- to 6-quart pot, melt butter and add flour, mixing thoroughly until golden brown. Quickly add onion, green pepper, celery and garlic, stirring frequently until vegetables are glazed and tender. Add remaining ingredients except water and mix thoroughly. Mix in cold water and bring to a boil, then reduce heat and simmer for 12 minutes. Before serving, reheat slowly over low heat and gradually add 1 to 2 cups hot water to provide gravy. Serve over rice.

Serves 4-6

Créole Chicken

The addition of brown sugar, raisins and okra to a basic Creole sauce makes this new version even more sumptuous than other classic recipes.

- 4 tablespoons vegetable oil
- 2 cups onions, chopped
- ¾ cup green pepper, chopped
- 2 cloves garlic, minced
- ½ teaspoon paprika
- 1 1-pound 12-ounce can whole tomatoes
- 1 bay leaf
- ½ teaspoon salt
- ¼ teaspoon ground pepper
- 2 tablespoons fresh parsley, chopped
- 1 tablespoon brown sugar
- 2 tablespoons raisins
- ¼ pound okra*
- 1 cup red wine
- 2 2½-pound chickens (cut in 8ths)
- 1 teaspoon salt
- ¼ teaspoon pepper
- ⅓ cup vegetable oil
- 10 fresh mushrooms, whole

In a 4-quart skillet, heat 4 tablespoons oil. Add onions, green pepper and garlic and saute until tender. Mix with wooden spoon to keep from sticking. Add paprika. Cut tomatoes in chunks and add to skilled with liquid from can. Add bay leaf, salt, pepper, parsley and simmer over medium-low heat until it bubbles. Add brown sugar and raisins, mixing constantly. Cut both ends off of okra and discard ends. Slice okra into ½-inch pieces and add to sauce. Add wine and bring to a boil. Simmer uncovered while sauteing chicken, for 15 minutes. Yields: 8 cups.

Sprinkle chicken pieces with salt and pepper. Heat oil in Dutch oven or skillet and add chicken, browning 4 minutes on each side until no longer pink. If needed, add a little more oil. Blot the chicken with paper towels and put into a roaster skin side up. Pour half of the sauce over first layer of chicken. Top with remaining chicken and pour remaining sauce over the top.

Bake in 350° oven, uncovered, for 1½ hours or until chicken is tender. Last 15 minutes add whole mushrooms and cover. (Canned mushrooms can be substituted for fresh.)

*Fresh okra is preferred but if unavailable, canned okra, well drained, can be substituted.

Serves 8

Turkey with Pecan and Mushroom Stuffing

When you really want to make a special turkey, roast it stuffed with this expensive dressing. The crunchy pecans are far better than traditional walnuts or chestnuts.

Prepare turkey as for Main Street's "Turkey."

Stuffing:
- ½ cup butter
- 1 onion, minced
- 1 turkey liver, cut in small pieces
- 1 pound fresh mushrooms, chopped
- ¼ cup celery, chopped
- 2 cups pecans, chopped
- ¼ cup toasted bread crumbs
- 1 teaspoon thyme
- 1 tablespoon parsley, chopped
- ½ teaspoon nutmeg, grated
- ¼ teaspoon mace
- 6 eggs, hard-cooked, put through ricer or mashed
- ½ cup dry sherry
- 1 teaspoon salt
- ½ teaspoon pepper

Melt 3 tablespoons butter in saucepan, add onions and cook until soft. Add turkey liver and saute until lightly browned. Add mushrooms and continue sauteing. Add remaining butter, celery, pecans, bread and seasonings and continue cooking, tossing with a wooden spoon. Add eggs; moisten with sherry and add salt and pepper to taste.

Yields: enough for 10-15 pound turkey

Red Beans, Rice and Sausage

This new twist on an old New Orleans classic has made a main meal out of a side dish. Adding the sausage makes the big difference.

- 2 pounds dried red kidney beans
- 2 cups onions, chopped
- ½ cup scallions, sliced thin
- ½ cup green pepper, chopped
- 1½ tablespoons garlic, minced fine
- 2 tablespoons fresh parsley, minced fine
- 1 pound cooked ham, cubed
- 1 large ham bone, cut into 3 or 4 pieces
- 1 teaspoon salt
- ½ teaspoon ground pepper
- ⅛ teaspoon cayenne
- 2 whole bay leaves, crushed
- ½ teaspoon thyme
- ¼ teaspoon basil
- 3 quarts cold water
- 6 smoked sausages (Polish, French garlic, Creole)
- boiled rice

Soak beans in water to cover overnight. Drain the soaked beans in a colander and put them in a heavy 8- to 10-quart pot. Add remaining ingredients except sausage and rice and mix thoroughly. Bring to a boil then reduce heat to a simmer and continue cooking for 2½ hours, or until beans are tender. Stir occasionally and add small amounts of water if mixture appears too dry. While beans are cooking, pan grill sausages 12 to 15 minutes, turning frequently until well browned. Drain on paper towels and slice into ½-inch thick slices. Add to beans after beans have simmered for 1 hour. Serve over bed of rice.

Boiled Rice:
- 2 cups long-grain rice
- 4 cups boiling water
- 2 teaspoons salt
- 2 teaspoons margarine or butter

Combine all ingredients in a large saucepan and cook, covered, for 15 minutes on low heat.
Serves 6-8

Plantation Lamb Roast

Use a little showmanship here. Place the roast, surrounded by fresh parsley, on a large platter and carve right at the table. The inch-deep, seasoning-filled slashes are necessary to flavor the entire roast and also make for an attractive presentation.

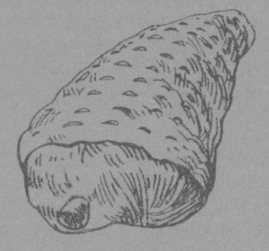

- 6½ pound leg of lamb
- 1 teaspoon salt
- ½ teaspoon cayenne
- ½ teaspoon pepper
- 2 tablespoons sugar
- 2 medium onions, chopped fine
- 2 cloves garlic, chopped
- 1 tablespoon Worcestershire sauce
- 3 tablespoons bacon fat
- ¼ cup all-purpose flour, sifted
- ½ cup vinegar
- ½ cup water
- 2 carrots, sliced
- 2 stalks celery, sliced

Clean lamb with cold water and slash meat one-inch deep at several places. Combine salt, cayenne, pepper and sugar and rub into lamb. Put onion and garlic into slashes with a drop of Worcestershire sauce. Gently coat (lard) the lamb with bacon fat and dust with ⅛ cup sifted flour. Place on a rack, bottom-side up, in a 400° oven for 10 minutes or until lightly browned. Turn lamb over, dust with remaining flour and return to oven for 10 minutes. Pour vinegar and water in bottom of pan and reduce oven heat to 325°. Place slices of carrots and celery across top of lamb. Cook for 2 hours or until tender, basting frequently. The pan juices make a superb gravy with the carrots and celery added.

Serves 8

Blue Bayou Monte Cristo Sandwich

A tasty Southern specialty that makes an everyday sandwich into an occasion. The light egg batter appeals to everyone and gives the dish a delightfully different accent.

Sandwich:
- 1 ounce slice white meat of turkey
- 1 ounce slice Swiss cheese
- 1 ounce slice ham
- 2 slices white bread

Make a sandwich with turkey meat, Swiss cheese and slice of ham. Be sure to place the Swiss cheese between the turkey and ham. Cut sandwich in quarters. Use toothpicks to hold sandwich together. Dip sandwich in egg batter and fry in 360° oil until golden brown. Remove toothpicks, sprinkle with powdered sugar. Serve with blackberry jelly and a fruit compote topped with coconut.

Batter:
- 1½ cups all-purpose flour, sifted
- ¼ teaspoon salt
- 1 tablespoon baking powder
- 1⅓ cups water
- 1 egg

Sift flour, salt and baking powder together. Add water to beaten egg and add to flour mixture and mix well.

Yields: 2 cups batter

Choux Fritters

Choux is the French word for pastries. And that's just what these light fried confections are—like a fried cream puff rolled in sugar.

- ½ cup butter or margarine
- 1 cup water, boiling
- ¼ teaspoon salt
- ½ cup all-purpose flour
- 4 eggs
- 4 cups vegetable oil
- granulated sugar

Melt butter in boiling water, add salt and flour and beat vigorously. Remove from fire as soon as mixture leaves the side of pan. Transfer to mixer bowl, cool slightly and add eggs, 1 at a time, beating after each addition. Heat oil to 375°. Dip tablespoon first in oil, then in batter, and drop batter into oil and brown thoroughly, about 5 to 10 minutes. Remove with slotted spoon and drain on paper towels. Roll in granulated sugar and serve hot or cold.

Yields: 3 dozen

Black Bottom Chiffon Pie

A chocolate-lover's delight, this super-rich dessert should be reserved for very special occasions. The chocolate custard bottom and the light airy topping combine beautifully.

1 10-inch baked pie crust (use "Apple Pie" crust recipe in Main Street section)

- 4 egg yolks
- ½ cup dark brown sugar
- 1½ tablespoons cornstarch
- ¼ teaspoon salt
- 1½ cups milk, scalded
- 5 tablespoons dark rum
- 1½ squares bitter chocolate, melted
- ¾ teaspoon vanilla
- 1 envelope gelatin
- 2 tablespoons cold water
- 1 tablespoon dark rum
- 4 egg whites
- ¼ teaspoon cream of tartar
- ½ cup sugar

Garnish:
- ½ pint heavy cream, whipped
- semi-sweet chocolate shavings

Beat yolks in top of a double boiler until light. Add brown sugar, sifted cornstarch and salt. Gradually stir in scalded milk and rum. Cook over hot water until mixture is thick and smooth, stirring constantly with wire whisk. Remove custard from hot water. In a small bowl, pour 1 cup of the custard and stir in melted chocolate and vanilla. Cool and pour into a baked pie shell. Soften gelatin in cold water and mix into remaining hot custard in top of double boiler. Add rum and mix well. Cool mixture to lukewarm, but do not let it set. Beat egg whites with cream of tartar and as they begin to get stiff, add sugar. Continue beating until stiff. Fold whites into the lukewarm custard. Gently spoon over chocolate custard in pie shell. Chill for several hours until set. Garnish with whipped cream and chocolate shavings.

Serves 8-12

Old South Pecan Pie

What's more Southern than Pecan Pie? Not much, that's why this New Orleans favorite has been revised for special attention here. It's so rich and candy-like, you'll only need to serve small pieces.

1 10-inch partially baked pie crust (use "Apple Pie" crust recipe in Main Street section)

- 4 eggs
- 2 cups dark corn syrup
- 2 tablespoons butter, melted
- 1 teaspoon vanilla
- 2 cups pecans

Beat eggs in a large mixing bowl for about 1 minute. Slowly pour in the syrup and continue beating until thoroughly combined. Beat in butter and vanilla and stir in pecans. Carefully pour into the partially baked pie shell. Bake in preheated 400° oven for 35 to 40 minutes until firm. Serve warm or at room temperature.

Serves 6-8

FRONTIERLAND

FRONTIERLAND—dedicated to the pioneering spirit of our forefathers—returns you to frontier America, from the Revolutionary War era to the final taming of the great Southwest. It's fun to visit and experience *Tom Sawyer Island,* Davy Crockett's explorer canoes, Nature's Wonderland, and the Wild West's rollicking *Golden Horseshoe Revue.* You won't forget sailing on the Mississippi riverboat *Mark Twain* or the three-masted *Columbia* on the "Rivers of America." These pioneering recipes will help you relive this hardy heritage.

Black Bean Soup

Although the name suggests a bland soup, it is actually robust and hearty. Don't be afraid to cook well in advance, so you can attend to other things, because reheating actually enhances the flavor. Goes great with thick slices of warm Golden Egg Bread, described elsewhere in this section.

- 1 pound dried black beans
- ¼ cup olive oil
- ¼ pound salt pork, cut into ½-inch cubes
- ¼ pound raw, cured ham
- 4 large onions, chopped
- ½ cup carrots, chopped
- 1 bay leaf
- 4 cloves garlic, quartered
- 3 stalks celery, chopped
- 3 quarts chicken stock
- 3 tablespoons meat glaze
- ¼ teaspoon cayenne
- 2 teaspoons cumin, ground
- 2 teaspoons salt
- ½ teaspoon pepper
- 3 tablespoons lemon juice
- ½ cup Madeira wine, optional

Rinse beans well and remove any foreign particles. Put the beans in a large bowl and cover with cold water. Allow beans to soak over-night (or if you prefer, drop beans in boiling water and cook uncovered for 4 minutes, then turn off heat and allow to soak for 1 hour).

Heat oil in a 5-quart saucepan. Add pork, ham, onions, carrots, bay leaf, garlic and celery. Cook over low heat, stirring occasionally until fat is rendered from salt pork, or about 20 to 30 minutes.

Drain soaked beans and add them to the pork mixture. Add the stock and meat glaze. Bring to a boil, reduce heat, add cayenne, cumin, salt, pepper and lemon juice. Partially cover pot and simmer over low heat about 4 hours, stirring occasionally until beans are tender and can be mashed against side of pan with a spoon. Add additional salt and pepper to taste. Discard ham and bay leaf. Put soup through a blender and puree. Return to saucepan and bring to a simmer over low heat, stirring constantly. Just before serving add Madeira, if desired.

Serves: 6 to 8

Garnish for soup is passed separately and should include:
- 1 onion, chopped
- 2 lemons, sliced very thin
- 3 hard-cooked eggs, chopped
- 2 tablespoons parsley, chopped
- 4 tablespoons ham, chopped
- 1 cup sour cream

Lettuce Soup

Instead of a salad to start off your fancy meal, try romaine lettuce in this unusual soup. Light and delicate, it's also an interesting conversation starter. A good point here is that this soup can be prepared in advance and frozen, as can any leftover.

- 8 cups romaine lettuce (approximately 2 heads)
- 3 tablespoons butter
- 1 medium onion, minced
- 4 cups chicken stock
- 1 teaspoon salt
- ¼ teaspoon pepper
- 4 egg yolks
- 1 cup whipping cream
- ⅓ cup sherry

Remove leaves from head of lettuce. Wash and pat dry. Chop fine and set aside.

In a 4-quart saucepan, melt butter, add onions and cook until tender. Add the chicken stock and bring to a boil. Add the lettuce, salt and pepper and cook over low heat for 15 minutes or until the lettuce is wilted.

In a bowl, beat the egg yolks, add the cream and blend thoroughly. Stir a little of the hot soup into the yolk mixture and blend slowly to avoid curdling. Stir egg mixture into the soup and cook over low heat, sitrring until the soup thickens. Do not let the soup reach a boil. Add sherry and additional salt and pepper to taste.

Serves 6 to 8

Pickled Tongue Paté

Ever made (or even tasted) a pickled tongue pate? If not, try this one. It's easy to make and impressive to serve. It's good as an hors d'oeuvre, on a buffet table as a spread, or on a bed of lettuce to begin a meal.

- 2 pounds pickled tongue,* cooked, room temperature
- 1 cup margarine, unsalted
- ½ teaspoon nutmeg, grated
- ¼ teaspoon cloves, ground
- ¼ teaspoon sage, dried and crushed
- 1 teaspoon fresh parsley, minced
- ½ teaspoon salt
- ¼ teaspoon pepper
- 2 tablespoons port wine

Put tongue through a meat grinder, twice. In a saucepan, melt the margarine. Add remaining ingredients to the margarine, then blend with the tongue. Pack tightly into a crock jar or deep pottery bowl suitable for serving, and sprinkle the top with additional fresh minced parsley. Cover with plastic wrap and seal with the crock lid or heavy foil.

Serve in the jar on a platter surrounded with fresh parsley, tiny tomatoes, gherkins and thin slices of rye bread, cut in half.

*Available at most ethnic delicatessens.

Pickled Beet Salad

Experiment by pickling the beets yourself for this salad. It's fun, easy and also versatile for garnishes and other uses. It's really healthy and refreshing, and can be substituted for the ordinary salad.

- 5 canned pickled beets, whole or sliced or fresh pickled beets (recipe below)
- 1 medium red onion, sliced
- 1 small cucumber, peeled and sliced
- 1 large tomato, cut in wedges
- 2 cloves garlic, chopped fine

- 2 tablespoons fresh parsley, minced
- juice of 1 lemon or 2½ tablespoons
- ½ cup vegetable oil
- 1 egg, hard boiled, chopped medium

Slice beets in half-slices and place in a large salad bowl. Add slices of onion, cucumber, tomato, garlic and parsley. Just before serving, toss with lemon juice and oil. Serve on a bed of lettuce.

Garnish with chopped egg and additional minced parsley.

Serves 4 to 6

FRESH PICKLED BEETS

- 5 raw beets

- water to cover
- ¾ cup cider vinegar
- 1 cup beet juice (liquid beets were boiled in)
- ½ teaspoon salt

- 1 cup sugar

- 1½ teaspoons mustard seed
- ½ teaspoon allspice, whole
- ½ teaspoon cloves, whole
- 1 1-inch cinnamon stick or ½ teaspoon ground cinnamon

Continued on next page

Cut tops off beets, leaving one inch of stem. Wash and cover with water in saucepan. Bring to a boil and cook beets covered for 1 hour or until tender. Drain and cool and the skin will peel off very easily. Set aside.

In another saucepan, combine vinegar, beet juice, salt, sugar and spices. (Tie all spices in a piece of cheesecloth before adding.) Boil for 5 minutes. While liquid is still hot, pour over beets and then cool. Refrigerate until ready to use.

Chip 'n Dale Parsnip Chips

Ever heard of parsnip chips? They can take the place of plain old potato chips, and they're better for you. Kids love them as an in-between snack or as a dinner vegetable.

- 6 to 8 parsnips
- 3 cups vegetable oil

Peel parsnips and slice crosswise as thin as possible. Heat oil to 375° and drop in a handful at a time. Fry until slightly brown and remove with slotted spoon to a plate covered with paper towels. Continue frying the remaining parsnip chips.
Serves 6

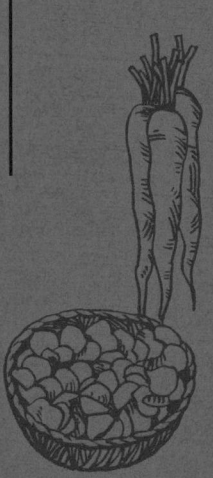

Frontierland Golden Egg Bread

What's so hot about this home-made bread is that while it's baking, your home is filled with its nostalgic, country-kitchen aroma. It's unusually light in texture, and there's nothing like it when toasted in the morning. Unused loaves can be frozen in plastic wrap, and will taste fresh-baked when defrosted and reheated.

- 2 packages dry yeast
- 2 cups warm water
- ¼ cup sugar
- 4 teaspoons salt
- ¼ cup vegetable oil
- 3 eggs
- 7½ cups sifted all-purpose flour
- 1 egg, beaten
- ¼ cup sesame or poppy seeds

Soften yeast in warm water. Add sugar, salt and oil. Blend in eggs. Add 3 cups sifted flour and blend well. Add remaining flour gradually to form a soft dough.

Knead on floured board until smooth and satiny, adding more flour if necessary so dough is not sticky. Knead about 5 to 10 minutes. Place dough in a greased bowl, grease top of dough and cover with a towel.

Let the dough rise in a warm place (above oven is a good place) until double in bulk, about 1½ hours.

Divide dough into desired portions. Roll each part into strips for braiding. Braid three strips together, sealing ends. Place braid in well-greased bread pan or cookie sheet. (If desired, cornmeal can be sprinkled on bottom of pan before dough.) Cover with a towel and let rise in a warm place until light and airy, about 1 hour. Brush with beaten egg and sprinkle with sesame or poppy seeds. Bake in preheated 375° oven for approximately 30-40 minutes, or until golden.

Yields 3 loaves

Pumpkin Bread

We'll stack this pumpkin bread up against all challengers. There's no big secret, simply the right combination of right flavors. Freezable, they can serve as unique house gifts.

- 1 cup vegetable oil
- ⅔ cup water
- 3 cups sugar
- 4 eggs
- 2 cups pumpkin, canned*
- 1½ cups walnuts, chopped
- 3⅓ cups all-purpose flour
- 1½ teaspoons salt
- 2 teaspoons baking soda
- 1 teaspoon cinnamon
- 1 teaspoon cloves
- 1 teaspoon nutmeg

Mix oil, water and sugar together. Add eggs and blend. Add pumpkin and continue to mix.

Sift together remaining ingredients, except walnuts, and add to pumpkin mixture, blending thoroughly. Fold in walnuts. Grease and flour 2 9⅝" x 5½" x 2¾" or 4 7½" x 3½" x 2¼" bread pans. Pour equal amounts of batter into each pan and bake in preheated 350° oven for 1 hour or until toothpick comes out clean. (Larger loaves take a few minutes longer to bake.)

*Fresh pumpkin, cooked and pureed, can be substituted for canned.

Yields: 2-4 loaves

Hot Marinated Artichokes

When it comes to artichokes, dare to be different for a change. The sauce is the secret here, along with the cooking technique. Serve it all by itself—not with your main course as is usual.

- 4 fresh artichokes, whole
- 3 tablespoons vegetable oil
- 2 medium onions, chopped
- 2 cloves garlic, chopped
- ½ green pepper, chopped
- 1 stalk celery, chopped
- 2 tablespoons parsley, chopped
- ½ teaspoon salt
- ¼ teaspoon pepper
- 1 teaspoon oregano, crushed
- 1 bay leaf
- ⅓ cup tomato catsup
- ½ cup red wine (or chicken or beef stock)
- 2 tablespoons wine vinegar

Prepare artichokes by cutting off stem on bottom and snipping off edge of each leaf, then cut 1 inch off the top (point) of the artichokes. Place each whole artichoke under very hot running water for several minutes then turn upside down to drain and set aside.

In a 6- or 8-quart Dutch oven, heat the oil and saute the onions, garlic, green pepper and celery until soft. Add parsley, salt and pepper, oregano, bay leaf, pepper, catsup, wine and vinegar. Simmer gently for 10 minutes, stirring occasionally.

Place artichokes, bottom (stem) side down in Dutch oven and spoon sauce on each artichoke. Cover and cook over medium low heat for 2 hours, basting frequently. Add additional wine or stock if sauce reduces too quickly and becomes too thick. Artichokes are done when a leaf comes out easily. Serve hot, spooning sauce over each artichoke before serving.

Serves 4

Stuffed Potato Jackets (Shells)

Emily Post aside, eat this canoe-shaped potato shell with your fingers. The attempt with a knife and fork is unwieldy. The homemade applesauce filling is the perfect match for the crispy, crunchy potato skin.

(SHELLS)

- 4 medium baking potatoes*
- 4 cups vegetable oil

Wash and dry potatoes. Prick skins with fork and bake in a 350° oven for 1 hour or until soft to touch. Remove from oven and, when cool enough to handle, slice lengthwise in half (or quarters). Carefully spoon out cooked potato taking care not to tear shell of potato. (The inside of the potato can be saved and used another time for mashing.)

Bring oil to frying temperature (375°). Drop one potato shell in hot oil at a time for 15 seconds until it starts to brown and crisp. Remove from oil immediately with a slotted spoon and place on a plate covered with paper towels. Just before serving, fill shells with applesauce. Garnish with mint leaf or sprinkle with cinnamon or nutmeg.
Serves 8

APPLESAUCE
- 8 golden delicious or pippin apples
- 3 tablespoons lemon juice
- ½ to ¾ cup sugar (to taste)

Peel, core and slice apples and place in a large saucepan. Sprinkle with lemon juice and sugar and cook covered on a very low flame, mixing with a wooden spoon occasionally. When just soft and tender, remove from fire and put apples through a blender or mash for desired consistency. Cool and refrigerate until ready to serve.

*Select potatoes oval-shaped so they can be easily cut lengthwise into "boat" shape.

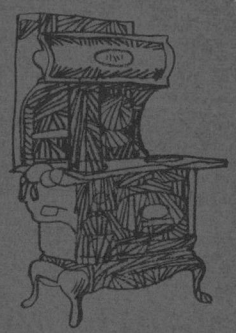

Tom Sawyer's Fish on Skewer's (Kebobs)

So why not a fish kebob? It may not be Armenian or Middle-Eastern, but it's every bite as good as a meat kebob. This can be a fun family meal or an elegant start for a company dinner.

- Juice of 4 lemons
- 1 medium onion, chopped
- 3 shallots, chopped
- 1 garlic clove, chopped
- 1 tablespoon peppercorns, crushed (or ½ teaspoon ground pepper)
- 1 bay leaf, crushed
- ½ teaspoon thyme
- ½ red or green pepper, chopped
- ½ cup tomatoes, chopped
- 4 tablespoons vegetable oil
- 1½ pounds halibut (or flounder), cut into 1-inch cubes
- 1½ pounds salmon, cut into 1-inch cubes
- ¼ cup sesame seeds

In a large shallow glass baking dish, mix all above ingredients except fish and sesame seeds. Thread fish on wooden skewers, alternating halibut and salmon. These are now kebobs. Place the kebobs in the marinade for at least 2 hours, rotating them every 20 minutes.

Remove kebobs from marinade and place on foil-covered broiler pan, and broil until slightly brown. Turn and broil until golden brown, taking care not to over-broil the kebobs or they will be dry. Remove pan from oven and roll each kebob in sesame seeds and return to broiler and toast for a few seconds.

Serve immediately on a bed of bibb or red leaf lettuce. Garnish with slices of lemon and thin slices of red or green peppers.

Serves 6

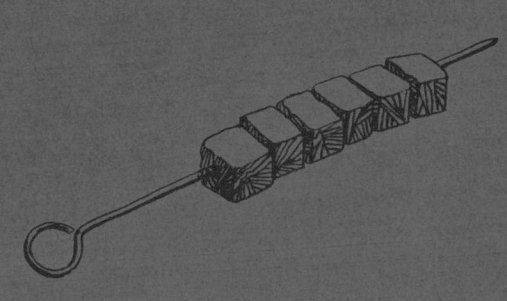

Vegetable Stuffed Chicken

You won't find this jewel of a healthful recipe in any other cookbook in any way, shape or form. It's authentic. The vegetables make this light stuffing different, and leaves you unstuffed. After chicken, try this delicious stuffing in veal breast, turkey, chops and Cornish game hen.

Stuffing:
- ¼ cup vegetable oil
- 3 medium onions, chopped
- 2 cloves garlic, chopped
- 8 carrots, grated medium
- 4 stalks celery, grated medium
- 2 parsnips, grated medium
- 2 zucchini, grated medium
- ¼ cup raisins, plumped
- ¼ cup red wine
- salt and pepper to taste
- ¼ cup quick oatmeal
- ¼ cup all-purpose flour
- ¼ cup cracker meal

In a large frying pan, heat oil and saute onions and garlic until soft. Add the grated carrots, celery, parsnips and zucchini and continue sauteing. Add the raisins, wine and salt and pepper. With a wooden spoon, mix in the oatmeal, flour and cracker meal in small amounts (by tablespoons) until stuffing is thoroughly mixed and moist. Set aside.

Chicken:
- 3 2½-3 pound frying chickens, whole
- 1 medium onion, sliced
- 2 cloves garlic, chopped
- 2 teaspoons rosemary
- 2 teaspoons sweet basil
- 2 teaspoons tarragon
- ½ cup red wine
- 10 mushrooms, quartered

Wash chickens inside and out. Fill inside cavity with stuffing and sew up cavity. On the bottom of a large Dutch oven, place sliced onions and garlic. Set the chickens on the onions. Sprinkle with remaining ingredients except mushrooms. Cover and roast in preheated 375° oven for 1 hour. Add mushrooms and additional wine if needed and continue baking for 1 more hour. Uncover during the last 30 minutes of cooking.
Serves 10 to 12

Indian's Beef Stew

There's no comparison, this stew is the most popular dish served at Disneyland. This is the actual recipe as served, and is a whole meal in itself. Wholesome and filling, it really hits the spot.

- 3 pounds stew meat, cut in 1-inch cubes
- ¼ cup vegetable oil
- 3 cups boiling water
- 1 tablespoon all-purpose flour
- 2 potatoes
- 1 pound carrots, sliced
- 1 onion, chunked
- 2 celery stalks, sliced
- 2 teaspoons salt
- ¼ teaspoon pepper
- ½ pound mushrooms, quartered (optional)

Brown beef in oil. Add boiling water, salt and pepper and simmer, covered, for two hours or until meat is tender. (Add more water if necessary.) Mix flour with 1 cup of liquid from meat pot until smooth. Add to stew and cook until thickened. Cook vegetables in steamer or in small amount of water until fork pierces easily, but vegetables are still crisp. Add to stew, then add additional salt and pepper to taste and simmer. Mushrooms may be added to pot during last 15 minutes cooking time. Serve over rice, groats or cracked wheat.

Serves 8-10

Skirt Steak Lollipops

Take advantage of this money-saving cut of meat by being your own butcher. Pound it, roll it, cut it, marinate it, broil it, serve it... and no one will ever guess that it's not as tasty and tender as fillet mignon.

- 4 pounds skirt steak
- wooden skewers (4½ inches long)

Place skirt steak on a wooden board and pound thin with a meat mallet. Starting at the narrow end, roll lengthwise as tight as possible, jellyroll style. At seam edge, push one skewer about ½ inch from side through roll and continue placing skewers one inch apart. With a sharp knife, slice in-between each skewer so you have 3 or 4 rolled "lollipop" steaks. Set aside.

MARINADE
- ½ cup olive oil
- ½ cup vegetable oil
- ½ cup red wine
- 2 cloves garlic, minced
- 4 shallots or scallions, minced
- ½ teaspoon ground pepper
- 1 bay leaf, broken into pieces
- 1 teaspoon oregano, crushed
- ½ teaspoon sweet basil, crushed
- ½ teaspoon salt

In a large, shallow, glass baking dish, mix all the marinade ingredients together. Place skirt steaks in marinade, cover and refrigerate for 4 to 5 hours, turning every 45 minutes.

When ready to use, place "lollipop" steaks under broiler or on a hot barbeque and cook, turning once, approximately 5 minutes on each side for rare.

Serves 8

Pecos Bill's Chili Con Carne

Your search is over for the world's best chili. This sensational recipe tops them all. If you don't believe us, prove it yourself!

- 2 tablespoons bacon drippings or vegetable oil
- 1 clove garlic, minced
- 1 small onion, chopped
- 1 small green pepper, chopped
- 1 16-ounce can tomatoes including liquid
- 1 16-ounce can chili beans, including liquid
- 1 15¼-ounce can red kidney beans, including liquid
- 2 teaspoons salt
- 1 teaspoon sugar
- 2 tablespoons vinegar
- ¼ teaspoon ground black pepper
- 3 tablespoons chili powder
- dash Tabasco sauce or cayenne pepper
- 1 pound lean ground beef
- ½ cup onion, chopped
- ½ cup cheddar cheese, grated

Heat 1 tablespoon of the bacon drippings in a large frying pan and saute garlic until golden brown. Add chopped onion and green pepper. Cover pan and cook over low heat until onion is translucent. Meanwhile, mash canned tomatoes in own liquid in a 4-quart saucepan or Dutch oven, then add chili beans and kidney beans including the liquid. Add salt, sugar, vinegar, pepper, chili powder, Tabasco sauce to beans and tomatoes and bring to simmer. Add sauteed garlic, onions and pepper. Reheat frying pan and saute beef in remaining bacon drippings, stirring with a fork to crumble, until cooked. Drain off fat and add beef to bean mixture in saucepan. Simmer, uncovered, for about 45 minutes, stirring occasionally. Serve in bowls topped with chopped onion and cheddar cheese. Accompany chili with saltine crackers or hot buttered tortillas.

Serves 4-6

Meat in a Loaf

No ordinary meat loaf this, the loaf here is a crusty bread casing. This takes time, in two steps, but it's well worth it. Bread and meat in one, it's an economical way to dress up hamburger.

- 2 pounds ground beef
- 2 eggs
- 1 medium onion, grated
- 2 cloves garlic, minced
- 1 tablespoon red wine
- 1 teaspoon Worcestershire sauce
- ½ teaspoon sweet basil
- 1½ teaspoons salt
- ¼ teaspoon pepper
- 1 tablespoon parsley, minced
- ¼ cup cracker meal
- 4 hard-cooked eggs, peeled
- 1 tablespoon yellow corn meal
- 1 egg, beaten
- 1 teaspoon sesame seeds

In a large bowl, mix with a fork all the ingredients except the hard-cooked eggs, corn meal, egg and sesame seeds. Mold into two loaf shapes and bury the two hard-cooked eggs, lengthwise, in each loaf.

Using recipe for Golden Egg Bread in this section, prepare the ingredients and allow dough to rise in a warm place for 1½ to 2 hours. Punch the dough down and divide into thirds. Roll out one of the thirds into a 12" x 12" square. Set the meat loaf in the center of the dough, fold dough over meat loaf and overlap dough, pressing together to seal. Bring side flaps together and overlap on first fold, again pressing together to seal. The meat loaf is now wrapped in the dough and should be placed on a greased pan which has been sprinkled with the corn meal, seam side down. Cover the loaf with a towel and let rise in a warm place for 20 to 30 minutes. Brush top with egg and sprinkle with sesame seeds. Bake in a preheated 375° oven for 1 hour. Serve immediately.

Serves 6

Orange Juice Cake

Close your eyes and imagine biting into a glass of fresh orange juice. Not really, but that's your first impression of this tart, moist, flavorful dessert. For company, top it with whipped cream.

Cake:
- ½ cup shortening
- 1 cup sugar
- 2 eggs
- ⅓ cup orange juice (not strained)
- rind of 1 orange, grated
- 2 cups all-purpose flour
- 1 teaspoon baking soda
- 1 teaspoon baking powder
- 1 teaspoon salt
- 1 cup sour cream
- 1 cup walnuts, chopped

Syrup:
- ¼ cup lemon juice
- ½ cup orange juice
- ½ cup sugar

In a large mixing bowl, cream together shortening and sugar. Add eggs and continue beating. Add orange juice and rind and mix thoroughly.

Sift together flour, soda, baking powder and salt and add alternately with sour cream to orange mixture in bowl. Fold in nuts.

Grease and flour a 10-inch tube pan and bake in a preheated 350° oven for 45 minutes or until toothpick tests dry.

While cake is baking, heat lemon and orange juice with sugar in saucepan. Bring to a boil and simmer for 5 minutes.

When cake is baked, remove from pan and place on serving platter. Pour syrup over hot cake. Serve when cool.

Serves 8-10

Recipe Index

SOUP   Page
    1900's Tomato Cream Soup . . . . Main Street   31
    Old-Fashioned Corn Soup . . . . Main Street   32
    Black Bean Soup. . . . . Frontierland   103
    Lettuce Soup . . . . Frontierland   104
    Jungle Mushroom Soup. . . . . Adventureland   49
    Disney's Clam Chowder . . . . Adventureland   50
    Shrimp and Oyster Gumbo . . . . New Orleans Square   85
    French Market Onion Soup . . . . New Orleans Square   86
    White Rabbit's Cabbage Soup. . . . . Fantasyland   13
    Won Ton Soup . . . . Fantasyland   14
    Astronaut's Cold Cucumber Soup . . . . Tomorrowland   67
    Asparagus Soup. . . . . Tomorrowland   68

SALAD
    Tuna Salad with Curry and Almonds . . . . Main Street   33
    Wooden Barrel Dill Pickles. . . . . Main Street   34
    Pickled Tongue Paté . . . . Frontierland   105
    Pickled Beet Salad. . . . . Frontierland   106
    Adventureland Marinated Eggplant . . Adventureland   51
    Zucchini Salad. . . . . Adventureland   52
    Br'er Bear's Okra Salad. . . . . . . New Orleans Square   87
    Mushroom and Pear, Vinegarette . . . . . . Fantasyland   15
    Chicken Liver Paté. . . . . Tomorrowland   69
    Natural Health Food Salad . . . . Tomorrowland   70
    Tabbouleh Salad . . . . Tomorrowland   71
    Stuffed Pear Shells. . . . . Tomorrowland   72

Recipe Index (continued)

BREAD

Pop-Up Bread	Main Street	35
Main Street Popovers	Main Street	43
Frontierland Golden Egg Bread	Frontierland	108
Pumpkin Bread	Frontierland	109
Pan au Chocolat	Adventureland	53
Fig Loaf	Fantasyland	17
Steamed Buns	Fantasyland	16
Prince John's Yorkshire Pudding	Fantasyland	19
One-Step Rye Bread or Rolls	Tomorrowland	73

VEGETABLE

Rutabaga and Carrot Puffs	Main Street	37
Macaroni and Cheese Souffle	Main Street	38
Potato and Mushroom Casserole	Main Street	39
Chip 'n Dale Parsnip Chips	Frontierland	107
Hot Marinated Artichokes	Frontierland	110
Stuffed Potato Jackets	Frontierland	111
Cantonese Fried Rice*	Adventureland	56
Tomato Stuffed Cheese Souffle	Adventureland	54
Spinach and Yogurt	Adventureland	55
Rice and Mushrooms	New Orleans Square	88
Sweet Potato Souffle	New Orleans Square	89
Eggplant and Tomato Pie with Tomato Puree	Fantasyland	20
Spinach Canneloni	Fantasyland	18

*Disneyland Recipes

Broccoli with Almonds, Onions and Garlic	Tomorrowland	74
Versatile Blender Sauce for Vegetables	Tomorrowland	75

FISH

Fried Fish Fritters	Main Street	41
Tom Sawyer's Fish on Skewers (Kebobs)	Frontierland	112
Rolled Sole with Muscat and Grapes	Adventureland	57
Shrimp Tempura*	Adventureland	58
Seafood Creole*	New Orleans Square	90
Pompano en Parchment Paper	New Orleans Square	91
New Orleans Shrimp Etouffee	New Orleans Square	92
Gravlax with Dill Sauce	Fantasyland	22
Goofy's Fish Mousse with Green Mayonnaise Sauce	Fantasyland	24
Cold Poached Salmon	Tomorrowland	77
Onion Crepes with Sour Cream and Caviar	Tomorrowland	76

POULTRY

Turkey with Apple and Raisin Stuffing	Main Street	42
Vegetable Stuffed Chicken	Frontierland	113
Chow Yuk*	Adventureland	59
Cornish Game Hen with Garlic Lemon Sauce	Adventureland	60

*Disneyland Recipes

Recipe Index (continued)

Blue Bayou Monte Cristo Sandwich*	New Orleans Square	97
Creole Chicken	New Orleans Square	93
Turkey with Pecan and Mushroom Stuffing	New Orleans Square	94
Chicken Turnovers	Fantasyland	23
Rabbit Provencal	Tomorrowland	78
Tomorrowland Turkey Kebobs	Tomorrowland	79

MEAT

Pizza	Main Street	40
Yankee Pot Roast	Main Street	36
Spaghetti Meat Sauce*	Main Street	44
Indian's Beef Stew*	Frontierland	114
Skirt Steak Lollipops	Frontierland	115
Meat in a Loaf	Frontierland	117
Pecos Bill's Chili Con Carne	Frontierland	116
Oxtail Stew	Adventureland	61
Marinated Pork Chops	Adventureland	62
Plantation Lamb Roast	New Orleans Square	96
Red Beans, Rice and Sausage	New Orleans Square	95
Veal in Foil	Fantasyland	21
Sweet and Sour Meatballs	Tomorrowland	80

DESSERT

Apple Pie	Main Street	45
Pie Crust	Main Street	45
Spicy Chocolate Brownies	Main Street	46

Orange Juice Cake	Frontierland	118
Far East Stuffed Figs	Adventureland	63
Schaum Torte	Adventureland	64
Choux Fritters*	New Orleans Square	98
Black Bottom Chiffon Pie	New Orleans Square	99
Old South Pecan Pie	New Orleans Square	100
Fantasyland Zabaglione	Fantasyland	25
Lacy Almond Cups	Fantasyland	27
Pear Tart with Dessert Pastry	Fantasyland	26
Fantasia Cheesecake*	Fantasyland	28
Apricot Sorbet with Chocolate Garni	Tomorrowland	81
Quick Blender Chocolate Mousse	Tomorrowland	82

Disneyland Recipes

Metric Conversion Chart

METRIC UNITS:
    1 kilogram (kg) . . . . 1000 grams
    1 gram (gm) . . . . 1000 milligrams
    1 milligram (mg) . . . . 1000 micrograms (mcg)

WEIGHT:
    Metric   U.S. Avoirdupois
    1 kilogram . . . . . . 1000 gm . . . . . 2.2 pounds
    0.1 kilogram . . . . . . 100 gm . . . . . 3.52 ounces
    0.454 kilogram . . . . 454 gm . . . . . 1.0 pound
    0.028 kilogram . . . 28.4 gm . . . . . 1.0 ounce

VOLUME, LIQUID:
    3.785 liters . . . . 1 gallon
    1.000 liter . . . . 1000 ml . . . . . 1.06 quarts
    0.946 liter . . . . 946 ml . . . . . 1 quart
    0.473 liter . . . . 473 ml . . . . . 1 pint
    0.227 liter . . . . 227 ml . . . . . 1 cup
    0.014 liter . . . . 14.2 ml . . . . . 1 tablespoon
                                4.7 ml . . . . . 1 teaspoon

WEIGHT PER VOLUME OF WATER:
    1 liter . . . . 1 kg
    1 milliliter . . . . 1 gm . . . . . 1 cubic centimeter
    1 quart . . . . 946 gm
    1 cup . . . . 227 gm . . . . . 8 ounces

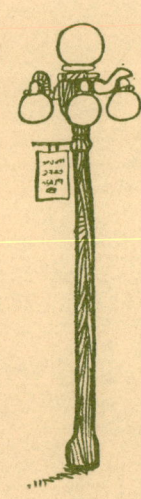

Table of Measurements

3 teaspoons	1 tablespoon
16 tablespoons	1 cup
2 cups	1 pint
2 pints	1 quart
4 quarts	1 gallon
8 fluid ounces	1 cup
1 fluid ounce	2 tablespoons
16 ounces	1 pound
4 tablespoons	¼ cup
8 tablespoons	½ cup
dash	less than ⅛ teaspoon